CIRCUIT RIDERS

MICK N. BAKER

Copyright 2025 Michael Baker

The moral right of the author has been asserted.

Some characters and events in this publication are based on real people and events… and some aren't.

All rights reserved.

No part of this publication may be reproduced, stored in a retrieval system, or transmitted on any form or by any means, without the prior permission in writing of the author, nor be otherwise circulated in any form of binding or cover other than in which it is published and without a similar condition including this condition being imposed on the subsequent purchase.

Dedicated to the brotherhood of Despatch Riders.

To Chris, Jess, Abbie, Felix, Evangeline.

For Mum and Dad

CONTENTS.

ENDRO

RED LINE FEVER

SEPTEMBER

BLOODY SUNDAY

CIRCUIT RIDERS

ALIENS

BYRON'S POOL

THE PROVERBIAL

CHAOS U.K.

THE BATTLE OF MIDWAY

WEST ONE (SHINE ON ME)

CLUNCH PIT

NO ONE IS INNOCENT

RIDERS ON THE STORM

WAIT AND RETURN

THE DAM

OVER AND OUT

'On Iron Horse he flies.'

Kilminster, Clark, Taylor, Lawrence.

'Looking for adventure in whatever comes our way'.

Mars Bonfire.

ENDTRO.

In front of me, the sun's rays drew a shimmering pathway across the surface of the English Channel. Seagulls careered in the blue skies above, while higher up, cotton wool clouds scudded in from the West. Inhaling deeply, I leant forward on the rail and felt the cool spray on my face. On any other day I would have felt at peace, at one with the world, part of the bigger picture. Not today though. It was like all the beauty in the world was for other people. Why? Probably because deep in the bowels of the ferry, stashed in the top box of my bike, there was a Kilo of cocaine. How did it get there? How did I get here? Well, that's a long story.

RED LINE FEVER.

Black Death's speedo showed me I was doing 140 miles per hour. The rev counter told me I was 1500 revs off the red line. I wanted to go faster. Needed to go faster. The need for speed was insatiable. Leaning forward I lowered my body weight onto the tank, twisted the throttle and felt a wobble from the back wheel. There was only one thing that it could be. I'd felt it many times before. Letting go of the throttle, I sat up, looking for a way through the thundering HGVs in the crawler lane. Seeing my chance, I dropped my right shoulder and cut in. Ignoring the fat bastard lorry driver's blasting horn, I slammed on the anchors and pulled up on the hard shoulder. The eighteen-wheeler surged past buffeting me. I gave its occupant a cursory two finger salute, then kicked the Honda VFR750 up onto its centre stand to check the back tyre. It was as I thought. I had a puncture. Flipping open my top box, I grabbed a can of Tyreweld and connected it up to the valve, hit the switch and watched the milky gunk shoot down the tube. Moments later, it started bubbling out of the puncture hole. It wasn't going to hold. Not this time; the hole in the dark pitted rubber was too big. Sighing deeply, I thought about my options. One: I could phone the AA and wait for fucking hours on the hard shoulder of the M6. Two: well, there wasn't one. Then, I had an idea. I wandered along the hard shoulder, sifting through the detritus with my motorcycle boots until I found what I was looking for. Picking up a 13mm screw, I paced back to the bike rolling it in my palm, thinking this could do the job. I took a Philips screwdriver from my top box, pushed the rusty screw into the spewing hole and screwed it home. Immediately, the flow of gunk ceased, but would it hold under high pressure? I emptied the Tyeweld and lo and behold, it held firm. Grinning to myself, I turned my attention back to the rushing vehicles and thought, it's time to get back in the race. No sooner than I'd put the bits and pieces safely back into the top box, I rocked the bike off its stand and hit the start button. Beneath me, the engine roared into life, shaking me up. I kicked it into gear, grabbed plenty of throttle, and looked over my shoulder for a gap in the endless convoy of thundering lorries. Finally seeing one, I let the clutch out and the bike shot forward, out onto the open road. Behind me, I heard another blast from a lorry, but this time I couldn't be bothered with a riposte. He could go fuck himself on his own time. Now back in the zone, I felt the rush of the wind, felt the awesome power being delivered by Black Death. People thought I would lose my bottle after the accident. Slow down. Take it easy. Be sensible, but it wasn't like that at all; nowhere near it. If anything, I'd become even more reckless. My feeling was, I'd survived, I'd walked away from it; nothing could fucking kill me now. A few moments later I was back up to 140 again. Now where was I, I thought? Oh yeah, it was time to unleash the full power of the engine, see what it could really do. Take it to the limit. Take me with it. In front of me, apart from the endless line of crawlers, lay an open road. I checked the mirror behind me to see if there was any filth around – there wasn't, it was pig free – all I could see were banks of cars disappearing. Performance Bike Magazine had written in gushing terms of the incredible power of the VFR750FK, so now it was time for the claimed 108 horses to have a proper run out; all this cantering was for fucking wankers. Again, I leaned forward, adjusting my weight accordingly, then I twisted the throttle and watched the clocks rising. Rising, rising... until I hit the golden 155mph. The rev counter told me that Black Death had reached her limit; I was red lining. My feverish rush told me I'd gone well past it. I thought, one mistake now and you're fucking dead. I'd never felt so alive. Coventry was coming up fast. Experience told me, the old bill parked up near the slip roads, or sometimes at the top on the roundabouts, watching for people enjoying themselves too much. So, I sat up in my seat, felt the rush of the wind smashing into my body and decelerated, taking the bike down to 70. Soon, I was passed the slip roads, and the coast was clear again, so I began to ramp it up. I was having the time of my life, buzzing like a mad cunt, enjoying myself. In reality there was no need to go so fast; I had plenty of time. It was 11 in the morning and the wait and return from Shell Southbank in my top box had to be in Liverpool by 3. So I kept it at a steady 90 for a while, but as I came up to another junction, a Yamaha FZR 1000R EXUP came ripping down the slip road. Perched on the tiny seat, its rider wore full race leathers; that was enough provocation for me. I tooted my horn, we exchanged a nod, and it was on. On the track, the Yam would make mincemeat of a sports tourer like the VFR, but we weren't on a track. This was the M6. Anything could happen. I kept him in sight until we hit the outskirts of Birmingham, then as the traffic built up, the cars slowed to around fifty and the Yam slowed too. Now I could use some of the tricks I'd picked up as a despatch rider. Soon I made up the lost ground and came up behind him as he tentatively made his way between the long lines of cars. I had one eye on his brake light and one on the drivers in front of us. One driver's head swivelled from the internal mirror to the wing mirror, then back again. My despatch rider's radar kicked in. I had seen it a hundred times before, so I hit the anchors dropping back, knowing what was coming next. The Yam rider saw nothing and carried on. In fact, seeing me falling away, he accelerated, trying to press home his advantage. Then the car swung right, changing lanes. My visor blazed red as the Yam hit the brakes. Its back wheel lifted off the ground. Dipping my shoulder left, I cut in between the car behind and hit the inner lane. Usually, you were pretty safe there. Not many cars wanted to change to the crawler lane, and unless the road was blocked, the

HGVs stayed put. However, if there was a junction coming up, you had to watch it; some drivers left it very late. Not long afterwards, the traffic stopped completely, so I gave it some throttle, got a bit of speed up. I must have been hitting around 50 when I saw the headlight of the Yam. He wasn't beaten yet. EXUP riders never were. Checking in the mirror now and again, I couldn't help but laugh when another dickhead pulled a right on him. Easing off the throttle, I slowed down, rubbernecking as he pulled up next to the driver-side door and started pounding on the window with his gauntlet gloves. I creased up again, thinking another racing bike fucked by the Black Death. Then sped off leaving the road rage behind me in my exhaust fumes. Thankfully, on the other side of Brum, the traffic eased off, and the road opened up again; I opened up the bike too. Soon, I was ton-up, leaving the urban sprawl of Birmingham behind me in the mirror, heading out into the countryside. Keeping my eyes on the scrolling tarmac wasn't so easy in the lush green surroundings, but I kept to my task. Cows passively chewed away on the cud in their fields, while I rinsed the arse off the horses. By the time the sign for Stoke came into view, I had forgotten about the EXUP and the easy victory; I was already looking for the next mug. Then the beam of a headlight flashed across my mirror. There was the toot of a horn, and the Yam edged up beside me. The rider gave me the thumbs up. Grinning back through my black scuffed up full faced crash helmet, I reciprocated. He nodded and powered up the slip road towards Stoke. There was never any real animosity between the riders; a burn up was just a burn up. Win or lose, it was just another part of the game. Manchester soon followed, then as I came up to Liverpool, it was time to find out exactly where the drop was. I raced up the slip road and found the nearest garage, which just happened to be Shell. I pulled up on the forecourt, switched the engine off, stretched my arms out eagle-like. I felt good, energised, ready for anything.

Inhaling deeply, I looked down at my radio hanging on my chest. The red light was blinking. For some reason I'd left it on. I was well out of range of base, so it was silent. Twisting the volume control all the way to the left, I turned it off to save what was left of the battery, then checked the fuel gauge on the VFR. No problems there, there was over half a tank left, more than enough to get me into London, then onto the Farm. Everything else looked good, the bike was sound. So I pulled the drop out of my newspaper boy's bag at my side and read the address. Soon I'd memorised it and chucked the A4 envelope back into the bag. Then I made my way up to the petrol station's entrance and saw the stupid 'NO CRASH HELMETS' sign. Exhaling irritably, I stopped in my tracks, dragged my full face off, and had a decent scratch at my itchy scalp. Seconds later, like they had a doorman, the door flew open, and an old bloke came out, his hands clutching a newspaper. He grinned at me and held it open extravagantly. Thanking him with a sarcastic, ingratiating little bow, I made my way inside. Then moved quickly over to the maps section, grabbed the map of Liverpool and thumbed it open to the index. Peeping over towards the tills, I was relieved that there were quite a few people waiting to be served. Experience told me I'd still better hurry though. People serving in garages could be right wankers when it came to the maps. Fuck knows why. Maybe it was company policy? Maybe they were just wankers? Whichever one it was, I had just found the address in the index when I heard the all too familiar.

"Er, excuse me? Excuse me, can I help you?"

"No thanks... I'm OK." I replied, quickly flicking to the map page.

Using my index finger, I traced the arterial roads from the motorway junction to the drop, but it was complex. I needed more time.

"Excuse me pal," the bloke behind the counter continued.

"Yeah, yeah, yeah, OK, OK, OK," I said distractedly, trying to memorise the roads, make the connections.

"This isn't a bloody library la, either buy it or leave," he moaned.

"OK. OK, keep your hair on mate. I'm putting it down now," I told him, not putting it down now.

In the simplest of terms, the drop was ten roads off from where I was, two rights and three lefts, right then left and then three rights.

"I'm not asking again."

"Well fucking don't then," I muttered.

"What? What was that? Right. Are you buying that or not?"

"No thanks, I just remembered I need a map of Manchester," I grinned at the soppy twat and left him in a mist of scouser swearing.

No time to reply, I strolled back to my bike and hopped on, thinking for fucks sake, why is he giving me a hard time? What is it to him if I glance at a map? It's not coming out of his wages, is it? It wouldn't be worth me buying it because I only come up to Liverpool a couple of times a month. I'm sure Shell can afford to let me have a free look at a map. After all, this fucking drop is for them. The bloke behind the counter still wasn't having it, he was gawking at me from the window with daggers in his eyes like I'd slaughtered his first born. Sighing deeply, I pulled on my helmet, hit the start button, gave the wanker the sign he deserved and roared off the forecourt in a cloud of smoke and fumes. I carried on the M62 towards Liverpool, then turned off heading for the leafy suburb of Belle Vale. Soon enough, I found the drop and waited while the recipient signed the documents inside, which took all of five minutes. Then I was back on my bike for the return journey to Shell on the Southbank. Before I hit the motorway, I stopped at another service station and grabbed a sandwich from the fridge. While I was munching away, I noticed there was a post box in the car park and toyed with the idea of sticking a first-class stamp on the envelope, so I wouldn't have to ride into London again. One of the bikers at Addison Lee, reckoned he'd done it many a time. He had got away with it too, but Addison Lee was a much bigger company than mine, Central Express. If I posted it, I probably would've got away with it, been paid £150 for the drop, but if we lost the contract through my actions, or in this case, inactions, I'd feel like I'd let the side down. Chucking the last piece of the half empty motorway sandwich in the bushes, I hit the start button, slid my helmet on and saw spots of rain on my visor. I sighed, looking skyward. Dark clouds were marching in from the west, then I felt a couple of droplets on my face. I thought why does it always piss with rain when I'm up North? It's the same country, isn't it? The phrase 'it's grim up north' came to mind. Oh well! Now a decision had to be made, I could put on my 'nearly waterproof' Rukkas, stashed in my top box, but the day was warm, maybe 18 degrees. If I dragged them on, I'd be baking within five minutes; they'd turn into my personal sauna. Then later on when I took them off, I'd be drenched in sweat, and soon afterwards I'd be freezing cold. Ever the optimist, I thought the rain might hold off, so I got moving, see how it went. A couple of minutes later, right on queue, the heavens opened with a vengeance. I was pelted with hail stones with such velocity that I had trouble seeing through my visor. Not the best thing when you're a ton-up, so I flipped it open. Immediately, the miniature balls of ice flew into my eyes, stinging them so badly, I couldn't keep them open. I was riding blind. Throwing my visor about halfway down made it bearable, and I gritted my teeth and carried on, but I eased off a bit. Not long afterwards, I was about to pull up altogether to put on my 'almost waterproof' Rukkas when just like that, the hail stopped. I rubbed my aching face, rammed my gloves into my red eyes, blinked a few times to clear my vision, then got back to it. To the front the road was clear, so I grabbed a handful of throttle, hoping to put some miles between me and the poxy hail storm. Out of all the weather conditions I hated hail the most. What was the point of hail? Rain makes sense. You can mix it with magic mushrooms for a brew up. Snow too, good for snowball fights and sledging. Both are useful in their own ways but what does hail do? Fuck all, that's what. It's neither one nor the other. Hail is snow for wankers. I thought, what's the betting that knob cheese back at the service station loves hail? Odds on. Now the weather had cleared, I made good progress going back down the A62. Then when I got onto the M6, low and behold, the sun broke through the pregnant clouds moving in from the south. Beneath me, the shitty hail that had bombarded me with such precision was melting away. It was beautiful now, glinting back at me, golden in the sunshine. With 150 odd quid waiting for me back in London it was quite literally my road to Eldorado. Close of play for the office types, or orifice types as they were known at Shell headquarters on the Southbank was 7 most nights. So there was no great hurry to get back, but still, I kept the speedo between 12 and 1 o'clock. I couldn't help myself, that need for speed was ingrained, it had to be done. No sooner had I passed the junctions of Manchester though, the open countryside with its multiple shades of green, wrestled my attention away from the blur of the ever-scrolling fast top. Not only was the view awe-inspiring, but the cloudburst had washed away the motorway's noxious fumes. Everything was so fresh, I breathed in hard, like I was part of an EXUP's ram-air induction system. Almost joined to me at the hip, Black Death was racing against time, unstoppable, ripping through the air, eating up the miles with ease. In the sky above, the sun's rays drew me southwards, marking the road to my prize, while all around me the fields held the addictive black fast top in place. Stoke quickly came and went as did Brum, but as I turned off on to the A1M, I began to relax, slow down, sink into the VFR's bench-like seat, start thinking things over. Being positive was a must; I always wanted to have that PMA, that positive mental attitude, think about good things, but sometimes my thoughts drifted back to the crash. How could they not? Sometimes it was impossible to stop them. I tried to keep a lid on it, but still they came. It was a Pandora's box. Every time it opened, something new came to the surface. The more I thought about it. The more I remembered. It was like the falling of dominoes. One memory knocked onto another, and a connection was made. Something else would reveal itself, something new would be thrown up. Good and bad. In the intervening years, I had pieced it together but there were a lot of gaps, particularly in the conversations I'd had; one conversation in particular, I was very keen to remember. Slowing down to a leisurely 60, I flipped up my visor, took in the ram air and let my thoughts drift back to the day of the crash. Clearly, I remembered watching the billowing smoke from the burning van twisting high into the sky, then the ground rushing up to meet me as I fell. How long I was out for, I didn't know, but the next thing I knew there was a voice softly calling my name. There was a blinding light as I cracked open my eyes. Then it was gone, replaced by a silhouette. The silhouette of a bearded man. He looked down upon me. He called out my name again. Then again louder. Fear ravaged my broken body. I was shitting myself. What the fucking hell is going on? I thought. Is this it? My time's not up yet. Is it? I'm not even twenty years old… I whinged internally. Then I realised it must be Hugh.

"Skinner are you OK?" He asked softly.

I was certain it wasn't the big man in the sky now, there was no way he'd be addressing me as 'Skinner'.

"Hugh… I'm OK."

"Can you get up?"

"Yeah, think so," I told him, not knowing it to be true.

Hugh carefully helped me up on to my feet. Then he put my arm over his shoulder bearing my weight, and we slowly made our way towards his Volvo. I was confused, dizzy, my head was throbbing, I was totally out of step with the world, but with his support I made it.

He leant me on the car while he wrenched the door open, "One minute you were behind me, the next you'd gone. I saw the smoke... the burning van. I thought..." he exhaled loudly.

"Come on," he said, guiding me to the door.

Never before had I felt so weak, nothing seemed possible, I was all over the place. Then as he helped me into the front passenger seat, the fire brigade shot past us in a whirl of sirens and blue lights. The next thing I knew I was in the A&E department of a hospital - the Lister in Stevenage, as I later discovered. I fell in and out of consciousness for I don't know how long. Unknown faces appeared speaking softly, cooing, trying to heal, then disappeared leaving behind only the burning overhead lights that clawed at my aching head. Suddenly Cerys' face appeared. For long moments, I wondered if it was a dream, an illusion. Then I felt the soft caress of her hand on mine. Cerys' eyes were red and wet like she'd been crying. She told me something about how the only phone number I had on me was hers. I couldn't remember if it was true or not, I just nodded dumbly, feeing the warmth of her hand in mine, hoping she'd keep holding it, hoping she'd stay until I was better. How long she was there for I didn't know; it could have been five minutes; it could have been the whole afternoon. I just didn't know. I couldn't remember anything about it: what was said, what we talked about, if we talked about anything important. If we talked about us again. One thing I did know was, this was the first time I'd seen her since I tried to get her involved in that stupid fucking threesome. The day I cheated on her; in front of her. The day I fucked up. The day I fucked up a good thing for good. If it was anything to go by, as she'd left, she told me she'd visit me again tomorrow afternoon, but I had been discharged the next morning. If I could have, I would have stayed at the hospital waiting for her to show up, but by the time the afternoon had come around, I was laid up on my bed back on the Farm. London was on the horizon now. I gunned the engine, thinking I was no closer to remembering the words that had passed between us. It could have all been so different if I hadn't been discharged. I shouldn't have been. Everybody I saw that day had asked me why I wasn't still in hospital. There was no way I had been ready to leave; I was still concussed. It was more about freeing up a bed for someone who was in a worse condition than me. Fucking Tory cuts. I flipped my visor down, giving Black Death a playful rev. It was time to get ready for the streets of London again. Time to re-enter the mad house.

SEPTEMBER.

On any other Saturday I'd be having a lie in, but this was September and September is the magic mushroom season. Renny was picking me, Brandon and Paranoid John up in his BMW at seven o'clock. I was hoping I wouldn't have to endure Den and Caitlin's early morning chorus today, but it was six o clock, and they were already at it. I suppose that's the way it has to be when you're sleeping in a room with your nine-year-old daughter. It was either that or nothing. Both Caitlin and Natalie – or Natty, as the corn blonde-haired little girl liked to be called – had moved in not long after Den. Whether that was the plan from the off, I didn't know, but knowing Den it probably was. He could be a cunning bastard could 'Dirty' Den, especially when there was something in it for him. Pete had been made up when Den had asked him if he could move in. He thought having Den around would make it easier for him to get his herb, but I knew differently. Impure and simple, Den was a smackhead; he would never waste his money on weed. Why would he? It hardly touched him. On the run up to Den moving in, I warned Pete time and time again; I was like a broken record, going on and on and on. Pete wouldn't have it though. He reckoned that instead of money, he would be getting paid in spliff every week. He just couldn't see it, he was clueless. Then again, he was always stoned, so it was no wonder. So much so, that Renny re-named him Cole, after Cole Porter's song 'Night and Day', because that's when he was off his gourd. Smack was a bigger worry for me where Pete was concerned. Badwitch, his old girlfriend, was already taking legal proceedings against him to get him out of her old man's flat. Pete always snatched up the solicitor's letters before I could get my hands on them, but it would only be a matter of time before the bailiffs booted the door in. If they found class A's in the flat, we'd all be fucked, fucked for good. Not only that, but on a personal level, if Den offered him a hit off the foil, would he be tempted? One day I asked him, and I couldn't believe his answer. He told me, 'He might give it a go, because it sounds like a good laugh'. It was at that point I threw my hands in the air and gave up. It was his place, his life. I had my own problems. A few weeks later, Den moved into the room next to me, while Pete moved his bed into the living room downstairs. Everything was fine for a while, and I was beginning to think I'd got it wrong, until Den started disappearing for days at a time. Renny told me where he was, he'd seen him. Most days he was around Aiden's place. He also told me he was back to his old game, back on the brown, but this time Den had put away his toolbox and was smoking his brown on silver foil - 'doing a foily' or 'chasing the dragon' as some people called it. Again, I warned Pete, but he told me, 'It's up to him, it's none of our business' and 'Anyway, he's not doing it here, so what's your problem?' Soon enough it became our problem though. One day, Pete asked me if I'd taken his *The Queen is Dead* album by the Smiths. I actually laughed. There was no way I'd have borrowed that. Not unless I wanted to play frisbee with one of Hillsey's dogs. For me, what happened was obvious, so I put Den's name forward, but Pete still wasn't having it. He was adamant that it wasn't him, after all, Den had been homeless when he'd let him move in; he wouldn't do something like that. In the end, he reckoned that as his place was the number one spot for a session on the Farm, and people were always coming and going, maybe one of them had taken it by accident. Maybe someone had pinched it, but it wasn't Den. A couple more albums disappeared, then it stopped. Then not long after that, Den stopped disappearing too, started hanging out in the flat with us, chatting. He showed us his other side, he was alright. It was a laugh spending time with him, he kept us up late, he had some great stories. Den had more energy too. He seemed, for want of better words, less sneaky. He was the bloke I knew before the smack took hold. Not long after that, Caitlin and Natty moved in. On the surface, Caitlin was a tough, no-nonsense type of person. You could tell she'd had a hard life, a violent one too, judging by the scar above her right eye, but now and again she showed her softer side. She was determined to move on with her life, not be defined by her past and she was going to do it by making Natty's life the best it could possibly be. She absolutely loved her daughter, and everyone could see why. Natty was funny, inquisitive, always wanted to learn and full of life. She bought a beacon of light into our drab surroundings. Everyone who met her loved her like she was their own. Checking the clock again, I saw it was six forty-five. I thought I'd better get a move on. Renny was always hassling me for being late and it would be worse at this time of the day. He was a right miserable cunt first thing in the morning. I hauled on my 501s, the only pair I had, threw on my raked-out Venom T-Shirt, then sauntered onto the landing. Passing Den's room I heard Natty giggling, it sounded like they were all awake now. Grinning at her infectious laughter, I shook my head and made for the kitchen to rustle up a bit of grub before the hunt began.

"Hiya Uncle Skinner," sang Natty skipping in, sweeping her long locks from her eyes.

"Hi Natty. How are you this morning?" I sang back.

"Don't know. I saw the sleep fairy last night, she was funny. She said if I didn't sleep, I would wake up with horns on my head... do I have horns?"

Squinting my eyes up, I perused her head.

"Oh my. Yes, you do!" I grinned, reaching forward to grab one.

"Noooo!" she squealed happily, batting my hand away.

"I do not. My mum says I'm beautiful."

I smiled back and shoved a piece of toast in my mouth, chewing it grotesquely, "Yum, yum."

Natty made a face, "Errrr... You shouldn't eat with your mouth open Uncle Skinner."

I cracked up laughing.

Natty smiled back, her big eyes creasing at the corners, "Uncle Skinner, can we do guitar lessons today?"

"I'm not sure. I'm going out, maybe tomorrow yeah?"

"Tomorrow? Why will it be tomorrow? Will you be out all day?"

There was an aggressive toot from outside.

"Yeah probably. Look, I'll see you tomorrow, OK?" I told her, getting a move on.

"Bye. Bye. Uncle Skinner."

"See ya, have a nice day."

Nonchalantly, I strolled up the yard behind my block towards the waiting car, taking in the early morning air. Before I piled in, I checked to see if Black Death was still there. You never knew on the Farm, but she was still there, under her tarpaulin, encrusted in a diamond-like frost. Brandon and Renny gave me a solid nod as I approached, then as I went around the red BMW, I saw Aiden sitting in the shotgun seat. He gave me a sarcastic smile, opened his palms up in a gesture that said, what? So I hopped in the back next to Brandon and we got underway.

"You alright Skinner?" Enquired Renny, revving the motor, his eyes searching me out in the rear-view mirror. "I can't believe you're actually on time. Did you get woken up by Den and Caitlin banging again?"

Everyone laughed.

"Yeah, some people use an alarm clock to wake up, but not me. I use the groans of a middle-aged bloke blowing his muck into his young girlfriend."

More laughter reverberated around the plush upholstery of the car.

"Alarm cock," sniggered Brandon.

Aiden leant around, "Have you seen Den's new jacket? It's baaad man," he informed us.

Brandon snorted, "Why's he wearing it then?"

"No, no, it's baaad like Michael Jackson bad."

Renny shook his head despondently, "Michael fucking Jackson? Are you sure mate?"

"Oh yeah, yeah, of course. You lot! Ha, just because you like music nobody else likes, you think you're better than anyone else."

Renny's eyes sought me out in the mirror again and we exchanged a look of wonder. Renny had little time for Aiden. Sure, Paranoid John was a pain in the arse at the best of times, but I couldn't believe that Renny would choose Aiden over him.

"Where's Paranoid John then?" I asked, hoping the Wacko Jacko fan would get the message.

Direct hit, he straightened up in his seat.

"He's doing his memoirs," Brandon grinned.

"It was in 1965, two years before 1967, six years after 1959, ten years before 1975," droned Renny, stamping down on the accelerator.

Snorting, I threw my head back and joined in. "It was five years after I rode a pig around Trafalgar Square nude, thinking it was Joanna Lumley."

Aiden shifted in his seat, "No, no, leave it out, the sixties were baaadd man, especially with all the birds. They'd just got the pill. They'd never say no, I tell you I was there, it was …"

Exhaling, I deflated in my seat, thinking this is going to be a long fucking journey.

Renny made good time down the A10, came off at the Turnford College junction, then back along the A1010 and finally turned left into Church Lane. On one side of the road, there was a pavilion with a football or cricket pitch depending on the time of the year. On the other, a massive cow field, where the Psilocybin shrooms grew from spores laying deep under the soft soil. Every year they'd come up, pop their little white caps up in the early morning sunlight, and every year we'd be there ready to pluck them, bag them, take them back to our houses and have a brew up. Sometimes the old bill would put in an appearance too, sniffing about. Normally, they'd just drive by, giving people the evil eye, but there must have been a change in Police policy, because during the last season a couple of my mates had been nicked for possession. One of them had been seen puffing weed and the other had been caught with a big bulging bag of shrooms. The smoker had been let off with a caution, but the Shroomeister's case was still on going. The law was as clear as mud when it came to magic mushrooms. It was legal to pick them but not to prepare them, which was stupid when you considered it. If someone got nicked picking them, then by the time they went to court, they'd have dried out and therefore be prepared. Everyone was watchful when we left the relative safety of the overflowing pavilion car park and made our way into the cow field. Even Aiden had shut up going on about the fucking sixties and all the stoned teenagers having this amazing, glorious, uncomplicated sex. By the way he was going on, it sounded like everyone had got plenty, everyone apart from him; he'd got fuck all. Brandon led the way into the misty field; beneath our feet, the grass sparkled with the early morning dew that washed our DMs clean as we walked. Within half an hour we'd scoured all the known areas, but with three other groups of shroom hunters on site, pickings were slim. Brandon knew a few other places, but even after another hour of sifting through the long grass, the count was still low. Between us we probably had about 50, which wasn't enough for a proper brew. So we did what we always did, we picked any mushroom that looked similar. The rule of thumb being, if they were white underneath the cap even if they weren't psychedelic, they were still edible. Soon, we all had a decent amount in our bags. Then reasonably satisfied with our haul, we made our way back to the car park where we found Doggy pulling up in his mum's dark blue Polo.

"You alright Doggy? Come for the football?" I laughed, pointing to the match in progress.

Doggy creased up, "Yes, I support Mushroom FC, FC stands for Fungi Cap," he gibbered back.

"Well, yeah, of course it does Doggy," I returned his laugh.

"Is there any over there?" He enquired hopefully, smiling at his mates Peter and his taller brother Tall Paul, as they joined us.

"Not much mate. We've only got enough for a couple of brew ups."

"Bloody hell Doggy, I told you we needed to get here earlier," moaned Tall Paul, pulling a bent up spliff from his Luftwaffe jacket pocket.

"If you'd got up when we'd planned, we could have picked them off the football pitch before the match started."

Everyone gaped at him.

"Football pitch? Where?" I asked.

Placing the spliff firmly between his lips, he pointed at the match in progress, "They're in the penalty area."

A few seconds later we were all crowding around the back of the goal waiting for the ball to go up the other end. It was taking ages though; one team was totally dominating the game. No doubt we were rooting for the underdogs, but they were playing like Doggy's FC Fungi Cap. Even as far away as I was, I could see the little white caps quite clearly. They were being ground into mush by the marauding football boots. It was fucking heartbreaking. Everyone else must have been feeling it too, because when a rotund defender hoofed the ball up the pitch, we all cheered and went into action. It was like the pitch invasion of 1966 that Aiden had been waffling on about in the car, but we weren't celebrating a victory, we were hoovering up the shroomies left right and centre. I couldn't get them into my bag quick enough. By the time the ball came back down the pitch, the pitch invasion was over, which was probably a good thing, because there were twenty-two blokes giving us the evil eye as we passed over the touchline. Back in the car park, before we said our goodbyes, Doggy told me his parents were out of the country until Christmas and if I wanted to pop in for a smoke, I was more than welcome. He said I could stay over if I wanted to. Doggy was alright like that. I thought it would be good to wake up in the morning to the sound of birds singing back in the village, rather than hear Den going through his vinegar strokes back on the Farm.

"Cheers Doggy, that sounds like a laugh. I will do mate," I thanked him, and we drove off in our separate directions.

On the way back, Brandon told us that Robbo and Trace had taken the kids out for the day, and that Hillsey and the pack would be the only ones in at Lenny the Lamp's. It sounded good to me. Sounded good to everyone, everyone apart from Aiden who reckoned we should do it back at mine. I knew the cunt was winding me up. He knew how I felt about doing drugs in front of kids, particularly Natty, but he kept on gnawing away until I said, 'Nah, you fucking melt, it's a baaad idea.' The car erupted in laughter. That shut him up. By the time we got to Lenny's it was around noon time. Barging the BM's solid door open, glad to be away from Wacko Jacko, I stepped out, looked up and took in the day. In the words of the Church of England, it was all bright and beautiful, light and wonderful. It was the perfect day for a brew.

"Come on Skinner, let's get the shroomies done, then it'll look even better," laughed Brandon.

"This is going to be baaad man," enthused Aiden, as we strolled through the yard at the front of Lenny's.

"Yeah, baaad!" I mimicked the fucking dildo.

One more of them and I was going to kick his arse all the way to Neverland, the fucking Jacko Wacko. Aiden gave me a sideways glance while Renny and Brandon grinned back at me, shaking their heads in unison. Hillsey was in the kitchen with his hounds when we trooped in swinging our bags of shroomies. It was feeding time at Lenny's. The pack were crowded around a decaying frying pan full of dog biscuits on the filth encrusted floor. Stinky Terrier bobbed his head up from the scrum to see who the visitors were, saw Renny, then growled and lunged forwards, taking a running jump at him. Hillsey must have been expecting Renny to drop in as Stinky Terrier was still on his string. He grabbed the red twine and pulled, heaving the raging beast out of the air. Then reeled him in. Stinky Terrier let out a yelp as he slid backwards across the lino, taking the packs attention away from the food and onto Renny instead.

Renny edged back, "I'm telling you for the last time Hillsey. You'd better do something to tame those fuckers, or they'll be dog biscuits."

"It's OK, it's OK," he cooed his errant canines, who soon calmed down. Then they turned their attention back to the feast.

Hillsey's zoo soon devoured their lunch, then Hillsey, with Renny's warning still ringing in his ears, shepherded them out of the kitchen into his room at the back of the flat. Then finally we got the brew on. Once the tea had brewed, we poured the soapy shroom laden water, into five mugs, brought them into the living room and sat back, sipping at the steamy concoctions, preparing for lift off. It tasted fucking vile, even worse than normal.

Renny took a sip and made a face, "You seeing Mia again Skinner?"

"How do you know that?"

"Ah, that would be telling, wouldn't it? No ... I was talking to a mate at a gig. He knows her."

"Oh yeah, who was the band this time? John Major's Septic Cock?"

Aiden piped up, "See that's what I mean about your bands, what kind of a name is that?"

Renny shook his head, he couldn't be bothered explaining our in-joke, "No, it was the Cro-mags, he reckoned you'd be up the Greenman looking for her, did you find her?"

"Yeah, I've been up there a few times."

Aiden snorted, "I bet you have you dirty cunt."

Not wanting to give him the satisfaction, I downed a decent draft of the brew, ignoring the taste and the twat.

Brandon lit up a spliff, "How's Carrie these days?" I haven't seen her about for a while," he eyed Renny through a haze of smoke.

Uh oh, I thought, this is not a good time to be asking that question.

"We're not seeing each other anymore," he laughed.

Aiden fell about, "You just can't keep a bird can you?"

Renny laughed again, but I could see he was getting pissed off. Carrie had started seeing someone else, an old boyfriend. Why, I didn't know, but Renny had confided in me. He'd been well cut up, and now Aiden was being a cunt about it. In fact, Aiden had been a cunt all morning and again everyone was feeling it.

Renny said, "I'm alright on my own, just one of those things I suppose, isn't it?" trying to brazen it out.

Aiden cracked up again, singing, "You are not alonnnnne."

"Ahhh, leave it out, not Michael fucking Jackson again," grimaced Brandon handing Renny the spliff.

Enough was enough.

"Nah, Michael Jackson is baaad, baaad man baaad," I taunted.

Aiden swivelled around in his seat. "Fucking better than the crap you like."

"Who do I like then, Aiden?"

"All that Judas Priest stuff, headbanger stuff."

I creased up, "Judas Priest? They're shit!! You're talking out of your arse."

Aiden leant forward belligerently, "Listen, Michael Jackson is the biggest selling artist in the world, he's got more gold discs than anyone else."

"So fucking what? The Tories are the biggest party in the country and they're a bunch of cunts."

Hillsey and Renny cracked up.

"He's got you there," grinned Hillsey, nodding at the logic.

"Bollocks," stated Aiden, his temper rising.

I snorted, "And Jackson's a fucking paedo."

Brandon put his hand up, "Alright, alright! For fucks sake, give it a rest you two."

Both of us nodded minutely and looked down at our brews. Bracing myself, I downed mine in one. It was disgusting, worse than normal.

Hillsey and Renny clapped in unison.

"Down the hatch, Skinner!" Laughed Hillsey, trying to follow suit, but he choked and puked the slop back into his mug, sending the room into fits of laughter.

Brandon knocked his back too, "Errrr, that is fucking rank," he said, slamming his cup down.

Nodding my head in appreciation, I turned to see what Aiden was going to do.

From inside his jacket a bottle appeared, "This is the way to fucking do it."

He took a sip of the beer, then the brew, "It's not so bad like that."

"Is it bad or baaaadd?" I smirked at the tosser.

Aiden swung on me again, his eyes blazing, teeth gripped together. He was fucking livid.

"Skinner, I don't know you, but Den says you're alright..." he trailed off, gripping the bottle.

"Den's a good bloke. No, sorry, I mean a baaaddd bloke."

Aiden flipped the bottle over in his hand, so he was holding it by the neck, ready.

Renny pointed at him, "Listen, don't start with that shit. If you're going to fight it's going to be a straight go."

Caught out Aiden put the bottle down, "You'll jump in, you'll jump in," he protested.

"No. I fucking won't Aiden, if you want a punch up, go outside."

Slowly, I stood up stretching, getting ready, waiting for the little cunt, but I soon regretted it because the shrooms were already kicking in. It felt like my head was touching the ceiling. Thankfully, Aiden stayed on his arse, tentatively sipping his brew.

"That's what I thought," concluded Renny.

Brandon sighed, "Everyone chill out for fucks sake."

"Come on lads, let's just enjoy the trip, this is stupid... Arrrrrhhhh," groaned Hillsey, leaning forward in his chair, clutching his stomach. "Aarrrrhhh Jeeeusss my gutssss aaaahhhhgh..."

"You alright Hillsey? What's up with you?" Brandon asked testily.

"I don't know, I feel sick. I've got to go; I'm going to lie down in my room."

"Really? It's not that shit, is it?"

"Sorry Brandon, I can't stay here... I- I'm going to puke," he groaned again, putting his hand to his mouth.

Hillsey hauled himself up using the arms of the chair and shuffled out of the room forlornly, holding his belly like he was about to give birth.

Renny laughed, "He's always like that on a trip. Bloody lightweight."

Brandon lurched forward clutching his stomach, then struggled to his feet and began retching,

"Oh Jesus Christ, what the …" he groaned between spasms, and picked up a wastepaper bin, then rammed his fingers down his throat, trying to empty the filth from his stomach.

Renny cracked up laughing, "What the fucking hell is up with you lot? This is great. I'm already getting some colours."

Brandon puked into the bin and chucked it aside, "Yeah, but you haven't drunk all yours Renny, nor have you Aiden," he groaned, wiping the spittle off his lips and looking down on Aiden's almost full cup.

Renny looked affronted and picked up his cup.

"Don't do it Renny, they're fucking poisonous," he said, making a grab for the bin again, then he rounded on Aiden,

"I bet you put them in, you daft twat. You wouldn't know psilocybin from a decent record. No wonder you're not drinking it."

"Oh, leave it out, Renny" he told him, putting his cup to his lips. "Here you go," he said tipping the noxious fluid down his throat.

Renny and me looked on satisfied as he guzzled the slop.

"When in Rome," grinned Renny knocking back his cup.

"Do as the Romans do," I finished for him, starting to feel queasy too.

In amongst the normal signs of an incoming trip, my stomach was cramping up. It was a weird combination to say the least, like experiencing heaven and hell at the exact same moment in time. On one side the light streaming in through the holes of the ripped curtains twisted into a glorious liquorice rainbow, dazzling me with colours, while on the other, my guts felt like I'd swallowed a four-pound bag of cement. Grimacing, I put my hand onto my bloated abdomen, caressing it gently, trying to calm the tremors. Aiden soon zoned in on my look of discomfort and started watching me like a hawk. I thought, if he sees me struggling, he could jump me here and now, so I turned my grimace upside down into a shit eating grin.

"You alright mate?" I asked sarcastically, fronting it out,

"Good shrooms aren't they?" I continued.

Aiden nodded cooly, "Well, I don't know yet do I? But Brandon's enjoying himself now."

"Is he?"

Slowly, I swivelled my head in search for him, taking in the room as I went. Chameleonic patterns of circles and stars slithered up the walls, throwing out every colour of the rainbow, while below, a thousand faces grinned up at me from the mud-stained, threadbare carpet.

"Where the fuck is he?" I sniggered.

Aiden cackled maniacally, raised his hand, and using his index finger he pointed to the other side of the settee. Easing myself cautiously up out of my chair, he came into view. Eyes bulging, mouth drooling, he was slabbed out on the floor, completely enchanted by the Artex ceiling. Aiden and me exchanged a glance and then we burst into manic laughter. There was nothing else we could do. He then moved forward and put his hand out,

"No hard feelings Skinner, Den says you're alright so that's good enough for me."

Even though I still had a bit of the weasel eye for him, I took his hand and gave it a decent enough shake. Now was not the time for a fight, I could hardly move. In that moment I didn't even know if I could stand up, let alone punch the Wacko Jacko prick's lights out.

Nodding I said, "Yeah don't worry about it. You're alright mate." Renny murmured something like, "Fucking bum boys," and the three of us who were left on Planet Earth descended into the giggles.

In the hours that followed, time stood still as we chatted about the visuals we were getting, then one by one we disappeared into our own worlds. I don't know where the others went on their voyage, but I got back to the twisting rainbow coming through the curtains. Incredible was the only way to describe it. I had seen those curtains many a time, and normally they weren't much better than the cloths I used to clean Black Death with, but today they were beautiful. Undulating and enticing, they gently wafted me away from the Farm onto a rainbow bridge at the far end of time, where sound and colour were the only things that mattered. I'm not sure how long I was off for, but when I came back, heaven had gone, and all hell had broken loose. Nausea and abdominal cramps had been bad enough, but the enchanting visuals had held it off, but there was no holding this off. My head was under assault. It was like someone was ramming a screwdriver into it, twisting it around, stirring it, mixing it up. Every now and again the screwdriver scraped against the inside of my skull, splitting the bone, sending shockwaves down to my feet. Rising slowly, I tried to hold my splitting head together, then I looked to the others, hoping for some help, but they were all slabbed out. There was no one here who could help me. By the look of them, they were all going through exactly what I was going through. I ran my fingers back through my long spiked up hair, then pressed my temples in an attempt to exorcise the screwdriver, trying to relieve the pressure. Nothing happened, so using the arms of the chair for support I hauled myself up onto my feet. There was only one thing for it: I had to get the fuck out of here. It was time to go home. Concentrating as much as possible, I slid one foot in front of the other, but it was hard going. It was as if the carpet was a mile below my telegraph pole-like legs, but I kept on telling myself it's not real, keeping the creeping insanity at bay. Suddenly it struck me how funny this all was, and I cracked up laughing then doubled over as I was hit by another series of cramps. Once I'd straightened up,

I steadied myself and took my first faltering steps out into the hallway. It was darker than the front room and my eyes struggled to see anything, but as my eyes began to get accustomed to the light, I saw Stinky Terrier skulking outside of Hillsey's closed bedroom door. He let out a soft bark.

"What's happened to you? You been locked out mate?" I sang at the little fella, sidling up,

"Here, I'll let you in," I said, playing the good Samaritan.

Edging the door open I peeped inside. Hillsey was lying on his bed with his pants and trousers around his ankles while his pack of dogs licked a brown paste off his erect cock. Slowly I swivelled my head, taking in the window, then the wall, then finally the light switch and I thought, Hillsey is lying on his bed with his pants and trousers around his ankles while his dogs are licking brown paste off his erect cock. Carefully closing the door, I turned and kicked into something. There was a muted whimper, it was Stinky Terrier.

"Shit, I know why you're out here."

Now I really, really, needed to get out of there, I was desperate. With new impetus I waddled to the front door, fumbled it open, and moved myself out into the daylight. Everything opened up. I couldn't believe how beautiful it was. It was like someone, or something, had turned the colour saturation up to maximum. This was what I needed. Clarity. Beauty. Inside me, the hell dispersed in the face of such great wonder, and heaven returned with its soft embrace. Even walking seemed easier now and I eased my way across the Ridgeway like I was walking on air, then something stopped me. That something told me I was being followed. I spun around. Stinky Terrier was trotting along about ten steps behind me.

"What are you doing? Go on home," I told him irritably.

He stopped and wagged his tail.

I snorted, "Go on piss off," then turned, and carried on.

In front of me, my block loomed large. With the sun behind it in the West, its silhouette was enclosed in a vivid burning orange fire. My sixth sense kicked in again. I turned my head. Stinky Terrier was still in pursuit; he stopped, then tentatively edged a paw forward.

"I'm not messing around. Go on piss off," I said kicking a foot out at him.

He froze.

"I'm serious. Go on, go home," I told him, and he backed off, "And stay away," I said, pointing back towards Lenny's.

Once I'd made it around the front of my block, I checked to see if the little sod was still about. Thankfully he wasn't, so I took in the treeline that runs down the side of Longwood Road. On a normal day it was magnificent, but today it was so much better; the sun's rays shone like beacons through the late summer trees, casting skeletal shadows onto the yards at the back of the flats. Glued to the spot, I must have been there for ten minutes, tripping out, on its intricate patterns. A couple of cars drove past, and I waved happily at the occupants, thinking that we were all part of this great expanse, this ever-unfolding beauty without end, this cosmos we all shared together, time and space in total harmony. Someone shouted out 'wanker' as they went by, then came the realisation that I was behaving like a complete bellend, and I made my way to the flat. Looking left, then right at my doorstep, just to be sure, I checked for Stinky Terrier one more time. Thankfully he'd taken the hint, and he'd pissed off, so I shouldered my way inside, straight into a shit storm. Caitlin and Den were arguing in the kitchen. It wasn't just a little tiff either, they were really going for it, tearing into each other. For fucks sake, I thought, can't I get any fucking peace anywhere? I'm off my dome here. Luckily the kitchen door was shut so I started for the stairs, then as I found my footing on the first step, I heard the name Kipper mentioned. Talk about scared sober. I stopped in my tracks, cocked my head, listening in. Years had gone by since I'd heard that fucking name mentioned, but even though they were buried deep, the memories still remained; me and Danny's search for weed in Harlow which was the catalyst for Little Dugs's death at his hand.

Caitlin shouted, "You fucking stole money off Kipper because you didn't think he'd get out of prison and now he is you want to borrow money from me to pay him back? What kind of a cunt do you think I am?"

No more was needed. I carefully made my way up to my bedroom and pushed the door shut behind me, closing out their slanging match. Checking the time, I saw it was 5:10pm, the day was fading fast outside, so I went to close the curtains, but I never made it because the cramps hit me so hard that I dropped to my knees in agony. I wanted to shout out, wanted it to stop but there was nothing I could do. Hell was back with a vengeance. The screwdriver was in my skull, turning, whisking, blending, scraping the bone, scoring it. Then my abdomen went into spasms. I grabbed *Sounds* the music paper to puke up on, but all I could do was dry heave. Bed was the only place for me now. Slowly, I eased myself down, keeping the newspaper close by, just in case. Then looking up at the damp ceiling, I tried to get the visuals going, but every time I started to get something, my eyes defocused and my head split open as the screwdriver dug deep. I tried again and again, but it wasn't happening. I wasn't giving up though. Deep down I knew I was going to be OK; it was just a matter of time. Time was the great healer, so they say - and it's true. Time would do it for me too. All I needed to do was stay calm, lie back, and in time my body would filter out whatever poisons I had ingested with the mushrooms. Then I'd be back to normal and tomorrow, me and my mates would laugh about it. Smiling to myself I thought I'd cracked it, cracked the code. Simple, it was all about time. How much of this shit had my body got rid of in the time I'd been in my room? Not much by the way I felt but still I looked over to the clock. It said 5:10pm. My smile fell away. I thought, 5:10? How can it still be 5:10? It was 5:10 twenty minutes ago, what the fucking hell is going on? Is this the day the earth stood still? Has time stopped? If it has, I'm truly fucked. I'm on this death trip forever. Downstairs, the argument ramped up another notch. First of all, I tried to blank it out, because it was just adding to the madness that was ravaging my head, but after a while, I found it a diversion and tuned in. I could feel every word being thrown between the two of them. Nasty, vicious and heartfelt, they were really going at each other. Any minute, I swore I was going to hear the slap of a fist on skin, but it didn't come. Then I heard the word 'pregnant', and I thought, surely, she hasn't got pregnant by Dirty fucking Den. The word came again, and I knew it to be true. She was.

Caitlin screamed, "You bastard," and the front door slammed shut.

Edging to the window I saw her marching through the yards, swiping at her eyes.

Den shouted, "If you're up there, Skinner, stay single, that's my advice to you."

"Yeah, whatever Den," I called back, crawling back onto my bed.

"Don't get lippy with me," he warned.

"Ah fuck off," I told him, then the tremors came worse than ever.

Doubling over, I felt like I had been punched in the stomach over and over again by Mike Tyson. Never in my life have I felt pain like that before. Den was a wanker but under the circumstances, it probably wasn't the best thing to have come out with, but there it was. So I propped myself up, watching the door just in case he wanted to try something. A few seconds later, the handle rattled. Then the door swung open and Stinky Terrier belted in and began to nuzzle my leg. Easing forward, I reached down, half expecting him to take a chunk out of my hand, but he didn't, he just wagged his little tail happily. Exhaling deeply, I scratched the poor little mite's filth encrusted neck. His tail wagged faster. He was loving it. I thought, now what? I can't take him back to Hillsey - not after what I saw. That was well out of order. The guy is fucking sick. Then I countered, no fuck it, he's not my responsibility, I haven't got time for a

dog. In a few months, there will be a baby in here too. Nobody's going to want Stinky Terrier around a baby. He's a nutter. He'd rip it apart. No, I'm taking him back. No, how can I? Truth was, I didn't know what to do because I couldn't think straight. My head was all over the place. If only I could think straight, get a grip on myself, then maybe I could work out what to do, but for now I needed something to focus on, to fix my fractured mind. In desperation, I looked over to my Technics. I thought yes, music is the answer. It usually was, so I propelled myself off the bed with my arms and shuffled over to the stack system. Not too concerned about what I was putting on, I grabbed the first record that came to hand. It was Venom's album, *Black Metal*. If I would have put that on, it would have taken me over the edge, so I dropped it like a burning sulphur. Instead, I opted for *Jahovia in Dub* by the Twinkle Brothers. I cued it up, turned it up and collapsed onto my bed. There were a few clicks, then music exploded into the room filling every corner. I couldn't believe my ears. It was like I'd never heard music before. Immediately, I was transported to a faraway place. I tripped out on mystic temples nestled in deep undergrowth on high mountains, on hanging gardens with waterfalls cascading down into cool clear freshwater pools. Nodding along, I was away; I was away for so long that the clock actually began to move, and the world began to settle down again. Then it vanished as the first side ended. Downstairs, the front door crashed with such ferocity that my bedroom window rattled, and I was back to reality. Back to reality at high speed. Someone was coming up stairs and my door was wide open. I looked at the gaping door then over at Stinky Terrier. An open door was basically an invite to any cunt who was passing to pop in and say hello. No way did I want that. I was off my dial. What could I say? What would I do? Paranoia spread like wildfire. Fuck off. Everyone needed to fuck off. Leave me the fuck alone. I froze, hardly daring to look. Then I glanced at Stinky Terrier. He casually got up, mooched over, stood up on his hind legs and pushed it shut. I creased up laughing like it was the funniest thing I'd ever seen.

"Whoa… nice one, he's a good boy, he's a very good boy," I chortled.

He looked at me, yawned, then turned his attention back to the door.

"What are you going to do next shithead? Turn the album over?" I gibbered.

The handle dropped downwards. I held my breath.

Stinky Terrier stood up, baring his teeth. "Grrrrrrrrrrrrrrrrrrrrr."

I heard a muffled, "Skinner?"

I thought, fuck off, fuck off, fuck off, I'm not here.

"GRRRRRRRRRRRRRR," went the plucky terrier.

The handle flew up, and whoever it was, thumped back downstairs.

Again, I fell about laughing, "That was something fucking special."

The little bag of wire wool turned, yawned again and got on guard duty.

"Well, I'll be dipped in dog shit!!" I said incredulously, scratching my temples.

"OK, you can stay for tonight. But don't get any ideas. You're going back to Hillsey in the morning, and that's the end of it, you got it?"

"Grrrrrrrrrr."

"Yeah, grrr whatever. And stay off my bloody bed, alright?"

BLOODY SUNDAY.

Sunday morning down on the Farm was not only about having a lie-in for the people who worked, it was the time to have a look at the motor, get it ready for the grind of the coming week. I would have been out there myself, but I was sleeping off the day before, and if it wasn't for some asshole's incessant knocking on my door. I would probably have slept well past noon. How long they'd been knocking I didn't know, but it must have been a while because the knock I answered to, rattled my window like Caitlin slamming the front door the previous night.

"Who is it?" I demanded, antagonistically.

"Pete. I need to ask you something Skinner."

"What?" I moaned, pushing up my aching stomach, stretching my lower back.

"Why is there a dog in the kitchen?"

From downstairs, Natty shouted excitedly, "Are we going to keep her?"

I cracked my first grin of the day, opened one eye and saw dog hairs at the bottom of my bed. So much for staying off the bed, you cheeky sod, I thought.

"Hold up, I'll be down in a minute."

Pete, Caitlin and Natty greeted me in the kitchen, while Stinky Terrier stood guarding the front door. I set about getting some grub and filled them in on how Stinky Terrier had followed me home after Hillsey had been cruel to him. Caitlin had pressed me for more details of said cruelty, but there was no way I was going to recount that part of the story. I was still trying to process it myself. Soon it was time to decide. Pete said yes, because he had always wanted a dog. For me again, it was an easy choice. If he wasn't going to be my sole responsibility and was going to be the house dog, I was up for it. Natty held her breath while Caitlin thought it over. Everyone could see her mum was just playing, building up the suspense for her daughter.

Finally, she said, "Yeah, come on, let's keep him."

Natty jumped for joy, her ringlets bouncing around crazily. "We've got a dog! We've got a dog! Ee aye addio, we've got a dog!"

"Calm down Natty, calm down for god's sake," laughed her mum.

The little girl looked up at her, beaming, then turned her attention to me.

"Is it time for my guitar lesson Uncle Skinner?"

Everyone cracked up laughing.

"OK, OK, let me finish my breakfast first," I told her spooning in the last of the soggy cornflakes from the bottom of my bowl.

Breakfast eaten, I was well up for a go myself, so I grabbed my Flying V guitar from my room and brought it down into the living room, where I found Pete folding away his sofa bed. In the corner of the room, the TV blared out some bullshit.

I said, "Pete can you turn that off man? It's guitar time."

"Guitar, guitar, guitar," sang Natty, skipping in behind me.

"Can't you do that somewhere else today? I'm watching Police 5," he said, lighting what I thought must be his second spliff of the day.

Natty said, "You shouldn't smoke, it's bad for you."

Pete ignored her and grabbed the remote control protectively.

"Watch what? It's the adverts mate," I told him pointing at the glimmering screen.

"It's on after them," he cried, turning the volume up.

"Oh what? Leave it out Pete we always play in here, come on shift your …" I trailed off as the volume drowned me out.

"Long haired dogs require enormous care of course and that includes nutrition..."

My head spun to the blasting TV, where a woman was filling a bowl with dog food.

"And that's PAL dog food. It's a top-quality meat in a rich brown sauce... Your furry friends love it! Especially the rich brown sauce..."

She put the bowl on the floor and a dozen dogs crowded around, devouring it. Snarling, I snatched the remote control from Pete's hand and extinguished the fucking TV screen.

Pete gaped at me, "Jesus Christ, what's up with you?"

"Nothing, nothing, er... I had a big night last night, that's all."

He gave me a puzzled look.

Behind him, Caitlin stood, her brow furrowed.

"Ooh, what's up with you, grumpy gums?" laughed Natty, breaking the tension.

Pete snorted, shook his head, breathed in a lungful of blue smoke, picked up the local paper and threw it up like a shield. Caitlin shrugged her shoulders and told us she needed to go out for a while, and then finally the guitar lesson began. Natty was a small nine-year-old and my Flying V Guitar had a solid wood body which made it heavy. Too heavy for Natty, so I would sit her on my knee and rest the guitar across her legs. It wasn't ideal, but it didn't put her off. Not one little bit. She loved her music, loved watching Top of the Pops, especially if there was a band that had guitars. She was a natural too, she picked it up easily; within weeks she could play A, D and E, which impressed me no end. Usually, we'd play for a couple of hours, but I soon found I wasn't in the mood. So, when Caitlin came back asking if anyone wanted to take the family dog for a walk, I volunteered, even though I had a bit of work to do on Black Death. Natty wanted to come along too, but Caitlin had other plans for her.

"Can I watch my TV now?" Queried Pete, sarcastically.

I snorted, tossed Pete the remote control and strolled into the hallway where I found Stinky Terrier on guard duty by the front door.

"You alright, Stink?" I asked the wire wool wolf.

His turret-like head traversed.

"Fancy a walk, then?" I enquired.

He jumped up and started running around in circles, his stubby tail going ninety to the dozen.

"That's a yes then, yeah?"

Then he jumped up and down, panting hard, then turned to the door expectantly.

"Hold on mate, hold on."

Even as a kid I'd never had a dog, never walked one either, but taking one out without a lead didn't seem like a good idea. Especially a little land shark like Stinky Terrier. Everyone seemed to have a dog on the Farm; he was bound to get into a scrap. Sending him into the front room, I had a root about in the kitchen and came out with a piece of twine. Then, I grabbed an old tartan neckerchief I used for biking in the summer off the coat stand.

"Oi Stink, come boy."

He bolted back. Carefully watching his every movement, I slowly slipped the neckerchief on. He couldn't have cared less.

"You're just a little softy, aren't you?" I proclaimed, and he nuzzled my hands, reinforcing the point.

"Come on then Stink let's go," I said, feeling the fresh air on my face as I opened the door.

Stink towed me straight to the bank opposite Black Death and began scanning the grass, reading the messages left behind by the other canines on the Farm. Now and again, he would stop, bury his nose, then take a couple of steps forward and cock his leg on what he'd read, then he'd trot on until he found something else of interest.

For me this was a revelation. I never saw the point in going for a walk unless there was something worth going to. Why would anyone go out and walk to nowhere and then walk back again? It made little sense. However, this was something completely different, we didn't need to be going anywhere, he was cracking me up just by the way he was walking. He had this 'come on then' gait, like his namesake, Stinky Turner, out of the Cockney Rejects. Stink eased off when we came to the alleyway between block five and six, commonly known as 'dog shit alley'. It was a good thing too, as there were so many turds about; I was hopping like I was crossing a river on stepping stones. Stink soon added his, then we continued into the kids play area at the centre of the Farm. OK, so there had been some vandalism, but there were only four swings, a slide and a rocking horse for the blocks on the west side of the estate. There must have been fifty kids living there. It was fucking pathetic to say the least. While I ruminated on the lack of local amenities, I slipped the string off Stink, and he bombed off into the overgrown hedgerows by the side of block eleven. Every now and again the bushes swayed aggressively, then there was nothing.

"Oi Stink! Come on boy, where are you," I shouted.

Nothing.

"Come on boy." I implored.

Still nothing, then suddenly he came pelting out of a bunch of stingers near the burnt-out roundabout, with a red ball in his mouth. Mouth hanging open, tongue lolling to one side, he dropped it at my feet. I sniggered at the mentalist, snatched the ball and lobbed it as far as I could. He was off like a rocket. Stink took ages to tire but when he did, I was glad. I couldn't believe how quickly the time had gone. In the west, the early autumn sun was dropping in the sky like a stone and I still had to check Black Death before another week back in the mad house. I collected up the ball, reattached Stink to his string and we got moving. Instead of going back through dog shit alley and risking the inevitable, we went through the blocks in the south of the Farm. Stink led the way, still sifting through the grass, reading the canines all-encompassing news. Suddenly he stiffened up and let out a low growl. Coming the other way there was a group of young kids. Ed Ridley, Ridsey's little brother, was at the front, his mates trailing behind. They were only twelve or thirteen, but they were already making a name for themselves on the estate. As we approached each other, I could see Ed weighing up the odds. Five onto one. The odds were well in his favour, so I was surprised when they passed me by, just dossing me out, but then they stopped.

"Oi, fore Skinner," Ed drawled, smirking at his mates.

One of them pointed at Stink and laughed, "Er, what's your dog wearing? It looks gay."

"Gay dog," echoed Ed, "Fore Skinner's dog likes it up the arse."

Stink shot at them like a cannon ball, scattering them like pigeons, but he was only after one of them: Ed. No matter what he did he couldn't escape. He zig-zagged left to right trying to lose his pursuer. He had no chance. Stink soon fastened his teeth on Ed's trailing jeans and brought him to ground.

He shouted, "Aaaahhhhhhhh!" and tried to kick him off.

I creased up, I couldn't help it.

"Get him off get him off," he wailed, spinning over flailing his arms wildly.

Stink clamped his teeth around Ed's arm and began shaking his head, digging deeper.

"Please, please, call him off Skinner, please."

Nah not yet, I thought, I've heard about you and your mates bricking the old people's bungalows on the north of the Farm. Then I thought. Can I call him off?

"Come on Stink."

He stopped; his head swivelled my way.

"Come boy."

Ed went to get up, but Stink wasn't having any of it. He bared his thin shark-like teeth and lunged at Ed's petrified face.

"NO STINK! LEAVE IT, LEAVE IT!" I bellowed, sprinting forward.

Ed batted Stink's head with the back of his hand, sliding backwards on the muddy grass, while I grabbed the mental hound and picked him up. He spun over in my arms, barking ferociously, then he saw it was me and calmed down.

Ed got himself up and started backing away. "I'm telling my brother on you; he's going to beat you up, telling him now."

"Ooooh, who's fucking gay now? Sod off you little prick."

"He's going to get his friend Kipper to beat you up too."

That was the second time I'd heard that name in as many days. It wasn't any easier to digest than it was the first time.

"Yeah, yeah, yeah," I told his skinny retreating frame.

"Fucking hell Stink, that was something else," I praised the little terrier while he too scrutinised the retreating Ed.

"Come on let's get back, I've got things to do," I told him, turning for home.

Stink nosed his way back into the flat, ran to his brimming water bowl in the kitchen and began to lap it up thirstily. Pete ambled in, watching the hound with red slitted eyes.

He drawled, "Whoa man that is one thirsty dog. Good walk?"

"Yeah. He got plenty of exercise," I returned, stifling a laugh.

Pete went to leave, then turned back Columbo-like, "Oh, yeah, yeah... I meant to ask man, you didn't happen to see Den on your travels, did you? He's gone AWOL again. Caitlin's worried."

"Is she? Well, he's probably back on the brown again."

Something registered in Pete's eyes, then his head dropped, "No way. No chance."

I scrutinised the well-meaning fool for a while, then with a sad shake of my head, I bent down, and ruffled Stink's neck, "OK Pete, whatever mate. I'm going to check the bike over. I'll keep an eye out for him."

In my early days of despatch riding, I had joined a motorcycle maintenance class at Turnford College to learn the basics. Not only was it a laugh as there were a good group of people there, but I'd saved myself a lot of money being my own mechanic. To start with, I had done everything from servicing to the more complicated stuff, like cleaning out the carbs, to changing the fork seals and brake pads. Truth be told, I would have done more but I was cautious when it came to doing the more complicated jobs. Some riders would boast about how they were going to strip their engines down over the weekend. Then you wouldn't see them for weeks. I thought it was fucking stupid. OK, they'd saved a few quid getting their engines back up to top performance, but they'd lost weeks of money doing it. My feeling after years in the saddle was, riding twelve hours a day was enough. Obviously, I'd still do the essentials, the bike had to be reasonably safe, but I would only check the basics now. Like the levels. Before I got to them, I admired the new back tire that Hammerax - the AA's bike repairers in London – had put on, after I had dropped off the wait and return on the Southbank. I snorted; it was fucking brilliant. It was so wide it looked like a car tire. In fact, the whole bike was fucking brilliant. It was black, sleek, aerodynamic and built for speed. It was a proper road rocket. Dreamily, I stood back taking in it's impossible curves until one of the streetlights pinged on above me, reminding me of the fast-dwindling daylight. Releasing the seat from its housings, I yanked it off and placed it on the pavement. The battery looked OK. Looking closely, there was a build-up of green-blue sulphate deposits on the connecting leads, so taking a bit of sandpaper I

scraped it off. Then I took my can of WD-40 and sprayed it liberally under the seat
to keep any build-up of moisture at bay. Potential mould thwarted, I bent down, undid the oil reservoir cap, re-dipped the attached dipstick and saw that Black Death had used a lot of oil during the last week. That wasn't good. It was a sure sign that the piston rings were on the way out, but there was nothing I could do about it, so I grabbed my oil can. I sighed, then looked up. Paranoid John was lolloping up Longwood Road in my direction. Again, that wasn't good. With his bullshit anecdotes, he could change a twenty-minute job into an hour one. I thought I'd better hide, but a little raise of his hand told me I was too late; I'd been spotted.

"You alright PJ?" I enquired, keeping my back to him, hoping he'd carry on.

"Thank you for asking. I'm very well thank you Skinner," he announced coming to a halt, not taking the hint.

"What's wrong with your mean machine?"

"Nothing PJ, just checking the levels."

"Ah yes, I remember the levels. The glorious Somerset levels. I went there after my first Glastonbury."

I sucked in a deep breath; I couldn't be bothered.

"Yeah, I bet, cooool man," I told him getting back to it, hoping he'd piss off soon. Very soon.

"Oh yeah, far out it was, man. It was a week before I danced naked at Jagger's gig in Hyde Park. Two years after I'd met Cliff Richard up a back alley behind Old Compton Street. The year before I invented the frisbee with Richard Branson."

That was it, I couldn't take any more.

"What? You knew Richard Branson?"

"Of course, everyone knew All-Bran. He was in Jagger's bed when Jagger shared a Mars bar with Marianne Faithful. I would have been there myself, but I was dropping acid on a boat with the Small Faces on the Serpentine."

"Wow man..." I said absently while checking the brake fluid.

"You know it man, it was like wowwww. It was the same week I jammed with the Yardbirds in Penge. Two weeks after me and Mark Bolan spray-painted his Mini purple, two years after I met Hendrix's dog Rainbow Bridge…"

"Please God hear me, I can't take this bullshit anymore," I mumbled to myself, searching the heavens for some kind of divine intervention, but there was nothing, just PJ droning on and on and on. Completely giving up on the man in the sky, I was just about to cover up my bike and piss off, when hallelujah! I saw Renny strutting towards us. OK fine, I thought, if there's no divine intervention from heaven above, then I'll take a heathen intervention down here on earth.

Renny cracked a grin at the waffling hippy gobshite, "PJ? Oi PJ? Hippy John's looking for you, he says he's got some shrooms in!"

"Yeah? I remember my first trip on the fungi flight path. I was with Syd Barrett on Grantchester Meadows, Byron's pool, the home of my ..."

"You better hurry man. He's brewing up at Lenny's."

PJ rocked back in his cowboy boots, waved his hand up like he was swatting a fly away, and plodded off in the direction of Lenny's.

Greeting my saviour with a thankful smile I said, "Cheers Renny, was that a lie?"

Renny nodded, watching the disappearing hippy.

"Is he getting worse or what? The dopey twat. If he'd have gone on for much longer. I'd have rammed this bottle of DOT 4 up his arse… Jesus."

Renny cackled. "I'm surprised we're not like that after that trip yesterday. Mate, I've never been so ill in my life."

Nodding my head while I packed my tools back into my top box I said, "Yeah, for a moment I thought I was going to die."

"What happened to you? The last time I saw you, you were standing in the hallway outside Hillsey's room, and mate... Your eyes bugged out! You looked like you'd seen a ghost."

I mumbled, "I wish I had of," into my top box.

"I came over to your place later on and that fucking hound of the bastardvilles slammed your door in my face."

I cracked up. "That was you, was it? Sorry man. I was well paranoid. I looked at Stink, then at the door. And he only got up and shut it. Just like that. It was like magic."

Now it was Renny's turn to laugh. "No not magic, Hillsey's always training his dogs to do stuff."

"A rich meaty sauce that dogs love" replayed in my head. Aaaaah stopppppp, I thought.

"Fucking is he," I spat.

Renny gave me a sideways glance, then shrugging his shoulders, he said, "I'm going up the Griffin for a couple of pints - what you up to now?"

"Nah, can't be arsed, I'll see you tomorrow mate," I responded, already walking towards the yards, "Oh, by the way, Den's gone AWOL... You seen him about?"

"Have I? He was in the Black Horse with Aiden at lunchtime. I got him a drink, but the tight cunt dodged out the pub when it was his shout."

"Dirty fucking Den," I muttered, before shutting the door.

Back in the flat, it was totally silent, which was unusual, because there was always something going on, some kind of racket. I'll go and see Stink, get a bit of grub and have an early one, I thought, nudging the living room door open. Stink was crashed out, lying on his back with his legs in the air, behind him on the couch sat Aiden with his arm around Caitlin.

"Right, time to go," he said removing his arm and standing up, "Don't worry, he'll show up soon enough, everything will be fine Caitlin." He glanced over to me. "You alright Skinner? Mad day yesterday, wasn't it?"

"Yeah, mad mate," I returned, watching him all the way out.

Not long after I'd heard the front door slam, I said, "You OK Caitlin, what's happening?"

Caitlin picked up a spliff from the ashtray, lugged on it hard, then blew it out like she was trying to blow her troubles away with it, "It's Den," she spat. "He's in trouble. I don't know what to do. I don't know where he is."

"Renny told me he saw him with Aiden in the Black Horse at lunchtime."

Caitlin frowned, "Renny told you that? Aiden just told me a minute ago he hadn't seen him, why would he say that? I don't know what to believe anymore, I'm trying to do the best for Natty. I don't need this right now."

"Listen Caitlin, I've known Den for a long time. You can't trust him; he's a dodgy bloke. To be honest, I don't know what you're doing with him, especially with Natty around. She's a lovely kid; she deserves better."

Caitlin straightened up. Her eyes bored into me. I'd gone too far.

"Den was with Aiden? Den's a dodgy bloke? What's your game Skinner? Natty's not your concern…. What are you after?"

"I'm not after anything; I'm just trying to..." I trailed off, thinking, I don't know what I'm trying to.

"Be careful what you say," she hissed, crushing the roach into the ashtray.

"Den's not the only one who should be worried about Kipper getting out, is he?" she asked, studying my face, "Is he?"

"I don't know what you're talking about. I've never met the bloke."

Caitlin threw her head back, "Then why did you try to score weed at his house, the night that little Duggen kid, got his head split open?"

"Bullshit, I've never even been to Harlow."

Caitlin snorted, "How did you know it happened in Harlow?"

"I've heard the story. Renny told me."

Caitlin laughed, "You're tying yourself in knots Skinner. I used to go around with Paige Stamp, you know Stampy's sister? He told us everything. The way you and your mate shat yourselves and ran off and let Little Dugs do your fighting for you."

"Now that is fucking bullshit. Stampy pulled a knife on me."

"So you were there?"

"Fuck this, I've had enough," I said furiously, stomping out.

"Go on then Skinner, walk away, but if Kipper finds out that was you... You won't be able to walk anymore," I heard, as I pounded up the stairs towards my bedroom.

"Bollocks," I shouted, and sat down on my bed, dropping my head into my hands.

There was no point in trying to reason it away. Kipper's kids lived at Lenny the Lamp's. It wasn't a matter of if he was coming back. Only when.

CIRCUIT RIDERS.

Central Express' dipole had a range of about five miles which was great for the riders living in central London. Marco, Muttley and Yacob could wake up, roll over and turn their radios on, and have breakfast while they were waiting for their first jobs of the day. Marco, the big Mexican who was on the run from his native country joked that, because he had five kids and his chances of having sex with his wife were limited, it was down to Graham our controller whether he 'fucked or not.' The rest of us bikers who came from further away benefited from this five-mile zone too, because sometimes we'd be paid to ride into work. Luck was with me this morning because on the way through Tottenham, I'd received a call on my hand-held radio to pick up from MK records in Camden NW1, going SW1. The route wasn't that different from my usual way into central London, but instead of carrying on all the way down Green Lanes, I turned right on Seven Sisters Road to go to Camden. Seven Sisters Road was always busy during the rush hour, but today it was even worse. It was fucking gridlock. Soon, I found out why, after I'd weaved through the stalled traffic to the one-way system, at the front of the Rainbow. One of the blokes doing the Knowledge on their moped must have been concentrating too much on his route board and not enough on the road, because he was now trapped between a bus and a car. Flustered paramedics clustered around him administering gas and air while a group of firemen tried to release him from the crushed metal. Even though black cab drivers and despatch riders shared a mutual dislike of one another, I couldn't help feeling sorry for the bloke, but stopping wasn't an option. What could I do anyway? Nothing. And I wasn't going to rubberneck. That was for assholes. Someone on a Honda CX 500 soon found a gap in the traffic and all the bikes - including me - followed him down the bike run. Left, then right, we weaved our way around the static cars through the diesel fumes, trying to put as much distance between us and the snarl up, searching for the open roads. Always searching for the open roads. As soon as I had got into Camden, I pulled over and had a cursory glance at my A-Z. I knew all the main routes by now, so it was only the last couple of roads I needed to look up. It was a small road off Bayham Street. A few minutes later I found the pick up, then noticed with some trepidation that Noel, another rider with Central Express' bike, a black Suzuki GSX 750 was parked outside the pick up too. Noel, a tall wiry Rasta, was a decent bloke. Sometimes we'd have a smoke together if it was quiet, which was great at any time of the day. The trouble with Noel was, he was a total burn up merchant. He always wanted to race, and he would never, no matter the circumstances, ever give up. I couldn't be arsed with it this early in the morning. Not only that, but it seemed pointless racing superbikes in the city. My feeling was that superbikes were for the open road, but I could never turn down a challenge. If someone, anyone, wanted a burn up, then as far as I was concerned. It was on.

"Skinner. How you going man?" enquired Noel, strutting over, disturbing my thoughts, "You picking up the SW1?"

"Alright Noel? Yes mate," I replied, heaving off my crash helmet, "Oh what, they haven't double booked have they?"

"No, I'm going WC2 wait and return."

Scratching my matted hair, I sauntered towards the entrance, grinning, "Thank fuck for that, that would be a shit start to the week."

"I'm going that way - I'll wait for you," he told me, beaming.

Nodding, I thought, oh for fuck's sake, that's all I need, a Monday morning race with the Rastafarian equivalent of Carl Fogarty. Dragging off my skid lid, I strolled into reception, taking my time and hoping he might get another pick up and disappear. I didn't know if it was the news of Kipper's imminent release or the shroom death trip on Saturday, but I really wasn't in the mood for it today.

"Hi, Central Express going SW1," I told the smartly turned-out receptionist.

She smiled a Rimmel London rouge smile and pointed with a deep purple fingernail at a box on the table next to her. It was fucking massive.

"I'm sorry I can't take that, it's too big, hold on," I told her grabbing my radio.

"Charlie seven, zero," I called, noticing the low battery light was flashing.

"Seven, zero?" responded Graham, Central Express' owner and controller.

"It's a van job, it's a van job," I told him, disgruntledly.

"Ok, roger that, leave it seven zero, I'll sort it. Drift in, drift in. Come into the city, it's quiet at the moment but there'll be something soon."

"Roger, Roger, my battery's going. I'll need to come into the office."

"Roger, Rog, come on in," replied Graham.

Palms up, I apologised to the receptionist again, who hardly noticed as she was too busy giving her perfect cuticles the once over and made my way back outside to find Noel still waiting. Expectantly, he revved his engine.

Not pissed off at all, I pulled a pissed off face declaring, "It's a van job mate, I'm going back to EC2."

Noel rolled his eyes, "Never mind, there's plenty more FS1E's in the sea," he quipped, viewing Black Death with distain.

I snorted and watched his bike lift off as he wheelied down the whole street.

"FS1E's in the sea, yeah good one. Fucking nutter," I muttered under my breath, kicking Black Death off its stand and getting underway.

Dropping south out of Camden using Eversholt Street, I took Euston Road, Pentonville, then when I passed the Angel, I turned right on Goswell Road and headed further south towards Central Express' base in Domingo Street, EC1. I felt the familiar shiver go down my spine as I stopped at the lights at the Percival Street, Lever Street junction. This was one of the many junctions I would never forget; never forget that day either. Never forget that whole fucking week. That was the week I had fucked up three bikes. On the Monday morning, I had blown a piston ring on my first despatching bike, a Suzuki GN400. I had been lucky in as much, that it happened on my way out of the Farm. Determined to get it back on the road as soon as possible so I could earn, I pushed it and free wheeled it the three miles to Rainbow's bike shop in Ware, to get it repaired. Luck was with me again as Richard Rainbow, or Clubhammer as we called him, had rented me another bike - a Honda CM 250 - while he fixed my GN. Two days later while I was racing a Honda VT500 on the Holloway Road, it blew a piston ring, just like the GN had. I couldn't believe it. It was like lightning had struck in the same place twice. Later that day, the bike and me were transported back to Ware by the AA, where I managed to rent another bike from the now impatient Clubhammer. This time it was the nippy little Yamaha RD350. On the Thursday of the three-bike week, I rode the Yam into London thinking, I'll take it easy, but it was so light, and it's pull away so fast, that I soon abandoned that idea and got back to burning up everything I could see. Performance wise, incredible is the only word I could use to describe the bike, but only if you kept the revs high. That's where I came unstuck.

I was shooting along Percival Street on the tail of a CX500, when the lights at the junction with Goswell Road switched from green to amber. The CX accelerated and rushed through on the amber, but when I tried to do the same, the revs on the Yam had dropped off so much that there was no acceleration. Next thing I knew, there was a car in front of me; it's shocked passenger's face gaping through the side window. I went headlong into its wheel arch. The bike bucked me over the handlebars, and I Super-Manned over the bonnet, crashed down onto the tarmac and rolled over a few times before ending up in a grazed heap in front of a looming London bus. People ran over to see if I was alright. The bloke whose car I'd hit, an older guy, was particularly concerned. I was soon back up on my feet, though, and for some reason I started laughing, which worried him even more. Once I had exchanged details with the driver and wheeled the crumpled Yam off the road, I found a telephone box and called Clubhammer.

"Hello, is that Mr Rainbow?" I ventured sheepishly.

"Yeah? Is that you Skinner? Don't tell me you've wrecked another bike? He enquired jokingly." Then hearing only silence. "Have you?"

"Sorry man ... it's er. It's a write off."

I heard some electrical buzzing, while he tried to digest this latest piece of bad news.

Eventually he said, "Fucking hell Skinner are you sure? I've been riding bikes for forty years and I've never fucked three bikes in a week."

To get my full weeks wages, or 'guarantee' as it was called, I had to show for work every day, so I had to ask, "Look erm, have you got another bike I can rent?"

"No," he spat, slamming the phone down, and that was the end of the three-bike week.

Smiling to myself, I watched the lights change on Goswell Road, thinking about Clubhammer's reaction when I picked my bike up that weekend. To tell the truth, it surprised me no end. He had this big grin on his face, like I had not only brought his bikes back safe and sound, but I had also had them serviced too. I thought, what a nice bloke grinning too, that is, until he showed me the bill. Four days of hard graft had earned me minus £178.67 plus VAT. No way was that happening this week. Not on Black Death, she'd have got me through that traffic light no problem. I'd have been long gone, and just to illustrate my point, I revved her up to the red, dropped the clutch and screamed off down Goswell Road, raced left on Old Street, then right into Domingo Street. It was time to see what the others were up to. Five bikes stood on the double yellow lines outside of Central Express. The two CXs belonged to our two Aus riders Chuck and Damo while the CM 250 was ridden by a Kiwi called Nev. Central Express had seen a lot of riders from the other side of the world. They would fly to the Far East or India and party like mad. Then fly on to the U.K. to work to get their funds back up before hitting mainland Europe. They were a great bunch. Muttley's C70 and Yacob's BMW were the other two. Adding my bike to the others, I gave Shirley, the girl who worked in the TNT office below Central Express, a wave with my crash helmet and clambered up the steep steps to the rider's room. Inside, it was packed out; all the bikers were perched on a long bench that ran around the back of the small room. One of the Aussie lads was telling a story, so after saying a quick hello to everyone, I settled on a tiny bit of bench to listen in.

"Hey Skinner, here, I'll start again just for you. I know how much you love those black cab drivers mate?"

"Yeah, I love the cabbies," I returned taking out my bacci pouch.

Muttley smiled through a row of broken front teeth, "You mean scabbies?"

Damo laughed, "Yeah, right you are mate. So, I was coming down Farringdon? And this fucking scabbie pulls a right on me?"

"What, again?" Interrupted Chuck.

Damo sniffed, "They're always doing it."

Puffing my first roll-up of the day, I nodded, "It's in the Knowledge - they train them to do it at Transport House. Forward the Strand. Left Kingsway. Pull a right on a despatch rider."

Yacob, our rotund Turkish rider, chuckled, "Sooner or later there's a black cab with your name on it," he intoned wisely.

Muttley pulled a shattered grin, "My grandad's a scabbie, I wrote my name on his cab. He doesn't get out much these days. I'll be fine."

Everyone cracked up.

Graham called, "Come on, finish the story," from the window into the radio room.

Damo smiled, happy to have the floor again, "OK, OK, so I pull up next to this pricks window? Gave him a right bloody ear full. But I didn't notice he was a big bastard. Until he got out. He wasn't fat either, he was built like a brick dunny."

"Oh, no mate," chimed Nev, "Did you cack yourself?"

"Fuck yeah, I thought, he's going to have my guts for garters mate. Then the passenger door opens, and this girl gets out. She's a Sheila. She must have seen the Aus sticker on my crash helmet. She gave him a proper dressing down. So, he's fair cringing under the assault."

Chuck made a chopping motion at his throat, "Ouch, yeah that's a bet Damo. He'll know not to mess around with a Sheila in future. Nobody should. I almost feel sorry for the prick."

Yacob chuckled again, "That's because you want to be a cabbie driver for yourself."

Everyone fell about.

"Bollocks," countered Chuck, "Tell you something for nothing, I'd rather drive a sodding cab than ride a BMW."

"Too right mate," grinned Damo, patting Chuck on the shoulder.

Yacob grinned, rolling his eyes.

"Alright, come on. Come on everyone, come on let's do some work," said Graham, handing a handful of dockets to the riders close to him.

I turned to Muttley. "You got that MOT for me man?"

"Give me a fiver and it's yours," he said passing me the document, "If you want a Tax Disc to go with it, I've got them."

"Yeah, brilliant man, no need. I nicked one off a bike last week. Went over the bike's number plate on the disc with Tippex. If you look closely, it's fucking obvious. But nobody will."

Muttley nodded.

"Nicked what Skinner?" Graham questioned dourly to a chorus of ooohhhs.

Everyone knew Graham used to be in the City of London Police, the ones with the special tit head helmets, but that was a long time ago. As far as Graham was concerned, if we got the work done, he couldn't have cared less how we did it or what we got up to.

"No, you misunderstand, Graham," smiled Yacob, "he was talking about his friend Nicholas, weren't you Skinner?"

Graham rolled his eyes to the ceiling, "Really?"

I chuckled, "Yeah St. Nicholas... I was talking about Christmas."

"Yes, his friend St. Nicholas," said Yakob with a butter wouldn't melt smile.

"OK Skinner, this is for you and your mate St. Nick. Here's a charged battery for your radio, and I've got some deliveries for ICC Banner Street going SW1, SW6, SW11 wait and return. Call me on the return there's more pick ups in WC2 pre-booked for later this morning."

Once I'd copied the office dockets into my rider's docket book, I trooped back down the stairs with the rest of the lads out onto the street. A few minutes and a few more laughs later, the six of us jumped on our bikes, started them up and with the raucous sound of high revs ringing in our ears, we dispersed in different directions and the day properly began. It was time to do some drops – burn rubber - get earning – get that sweet adrenaline hit. As ten, eleven and twelve o' clock all came and went, vanishing on my instrument panel, I thought to myself, yeah, I'm working around the clock: in time, MPH and RPM. Sadly, you couldn't go ton-up on the streets of London, but if you hit the 60s/70s, that would definitely get you through the traffic light traps which were mostly set at 50. Over the course of a day, those extra minutes made a huge difference to the amount of drops you could do, which meant more money. By the time 2 o'clock came, I was sifting through my used dockets and eating a sandwich outside of ICC in Banner Street, waiting for more jobs. Counting twenty for this morning, I had already gone over my day's guarantee by twenty quid, and there was still three maybe four hours still to go. No matter how many times I thought about it, I still couldn't believe I was getting paid - and paid so well - for doing this. It was like I'd been waiting for this since the band hadn't happened. Suddenly, I was disturbed from my ruminations by the radio on my chest squawking. Graham was calling, 'Charlie one, one, to Banner Street for a W1'. Charlie one, one, was Noel. Oh well, I'm more than awake now. I'm ready for him, I thought. Propping my legs up on the handlebars, I laid back across the bench seat, rested my head on my top box waiting for the inevitable. A couple of minutes later there was the roar of a GSXR hammering down Banner Street as the inevitable showed up.

"Noeelll, you alright man?"

He nodded back at me, jumping off his bike.

My radio squawked, "Charlie, seven zero, Charlie, seven zero, ICC fourth floor going WC1."

I confirmed with a "Rog," and Noel and me strolled into the building, chatting.

Banner Street was long and straight, perfect for burn ups, but instead of the usual boasting of who was going to beat who and whose bike was like Muttley's C70, we talked about the last Jah Shaka gig we went to at the Rocket. Noel left me in the lift on the second floor to pick up his drop, while I carried on up and collected my drop from the fourth. By the time I came back down, Noel was sitting ready on his bike, his eyes bugging out at me from behind his glasses. I hopped on, hit the start button and revved the engine up to the red line.

"You ready?" I grinned.

"I was born ready man," he told me and flew off down Banner Street in a cloud of burnt fuel, with me close in behind him.

Every Monday morning there was a market on Banner Street, which usually ended at 12, but for some reason it was still going on. I hit the brake and fell back while Noel carried on at a blistering rate through the stalls. Suddenly, from behind one of them, a pram appeared with a young woman pushing it. Without looking, she carried on out into the road in front of me. I thought, fucking hell, nooo. Dropping my shoulder, I threw the bike left and missed the pram by inches. There was a shout from behind but whatever it was, was lost in the screaming engines. Noel was way ahead now, so I grabbed as much throttle as I dared and made up some ground on him as he slowed to turn left onto Golden Lane. Then I was right behind him as he slowed to turn right on Fann Street. Kicking down into second gear, I twisted the throttle, leant the bike hard right and cut across the low pavement, taking the lead. He blasted his horn and came alongside me, nudging my knee with his. I swivelled my head around and put my fist out as we came up to the junction with Goswell Road and he left me hanging. His mind was on the burn up. Nothing else. Now this is where the race really begins, this is an A road I thought, seeing the green lights ahead at the junction with Long Lane. Kicking down into second again, I redlined it. Then watched in amazement as Noel passed me with his front wheel in the air. There was absolutely nothing I could do. The awesome power of the Suzi was going to win the day, but then for some reason Noel turned right at the lights, choosing to take the short cut through Spitalfields meat market. For the life of me I couldn't work out why. Got you now, I thought. The market would be awash with barrow boys ferrying the meat to the day's buyers. He would have to slow down, maybe even stop. Meanwhile I had a free run on the open A road. Aldersgate Street became a blur, then when I came to the roundabout at the corner of Plaisterers Hall, and was getting my knee down, a yellow van flew at me from out of London Wall. In a second, I heaved myself up and hit the brakes hard as the bike fish tailed and the van missed me by inches. The van driver blasted his horn, gave me the wankers sign and carried on into St. Martin's Le Grande, then turned towards Newgate Street. To say I was angry was an understatement, so when I caught up with him, I smashed my motorcycle boot into his driver side door. He swerved at me, trying to knock me off, but I was way too fast for him, and I left him in the slow-moving traffic on Holborn Viaduct. A few moments later I was at the front of the queue at the junction with Long Lane, watching for Noel. He wasn't there, which meant one of two things. One, the fucking bastard in the van had slowed me down so much that Noel had already gone past the junction, or two, he'd got caught up in the meat market as it had wound up for the day. It turned out to be number two. Noel appeared from out of the shadow of a huge freezer lorry and gave me a victory sign. Who the victory was for, I wasn't sure. Now, it was all about the traffic lights. If his switched to green before mine, he would be the winner. If mine did, the race was mine. My eyes flipped from my lights to Noel, expecting him to be doing the same but he wasn't. His yellow crash helmet was turned, focused on something behind me. Dragging my eyes off the infernal red light, I checked my mirror. Coming up fast, running in between the cars I could see the van driver. Big, with huge, tattooed arms, he was coming at me like a raging fucking bull. My eyes flipped to the red light, to the raging bull. Then to the red light, then just as the cunt got to me, the lights turned green.

"Fuck you, cunt" I yelled, giving him two fingers and left him choking in my exhaust smoke.

Clearing the junction I gave Noel the victory sign, signalling that it was my day after all, and powered off into WC1 to find my drop. Not long after I'd found it; a company on Great Russell Street called Rio PLC, I called in empty and slowly rode into W1 where Graham had plotted me up. HMV was in W1, so it suited me fine, as I needed to take a CD back. Vinyl was still my thing. I was still buying mainly dub reggae albums from Reckless Records in Berwick Street, but now and again I would buy CDs if it was an album I particularly liked. Compact Discs were supposed to be more robust than vinyl, but ironically, given its title, the Dead Kennedy's *Give Me Convenience or Give Me Death* CD I had bought had given me nothing but inconvenience. It was alright for a couple of tracks, then it would start skipping. Near the bottom of Berwick Street, there was a free parking rank for bikes, so I parked up, stashed my full-face crash helmet in the under-seat lock and made my way up to Oxford Street. It was its usual hive of activity. Hordes of shoppers crammed onto the pavements while hundreds of cars, taxis and red London buses crawled along at a snail's pace. HMV was always a bit further away than I thought, but then again, it was always like that in London. Everything seemed to be right on top of each other when you looked it up in the A-Z, but when you'd started walking, you found everything was miles away, especially if you were dressed in Rukkas and motorcycle boots. Finally, I sauntered into the huge shop. It was an amazing place really. Every type of music was available, from Mozart to Motörhead, to Prince Jammy to Prince. Everything was here, but it was all so ridiculously expensive. Not only that, it was the biggest tease on the planet. Every CD, tape, album and video would have been there for the taking if it wasn't for the security tags. Impossible to take off, the security tags were basically a magnetic strip of metal which would set off an alarm if you left the shop without it being demagnetised. To demagnetise them the shop assistants would use a small roller, running it backwards and forwards over the tag. It was simple and effective. It seemed to put off most of the thieves at Central Express, but I'd noticed how careless some of the shop assistants were with the rollers and I was hoping that carelessness would be in evidence today. I made my way through the hordes to the counter, spotted a roller, grabbed it, and dropped it into my newspaper bag.

"Yes mate?" Said the busy assistant turning to me.

"Oh, alright? This CD keeps skipping."

"OK, go get another one."

"Cheers mate," I replied nodding my head, then I weaved my way back through the throng of people waiting to be served.

On my way over to the punk section, I scouted out for any overhead cameras. I couldn't see any, which was strange when you thought about it. Me and my mates were always on the look for freebies, especially if we thought the shop was taking the piss with its prices. Soon I found what I wanted, and eased the roller out and demagnetised the Dead Kennedys first three albums then slipped the lot back in my bag. Then I took *Give Me Convenience or Give Me Death* back for the exchange. Nobody batted an eye lid; they hadn't even noticed the roller had gone. I couldn't believe how lax they were, couldn't believe how easy is it was, and I couldn't wait to tell Muttley back at Central Express. We'd have a fucking field day.

"Cheers mate," I said to the assistant and heaved my way towards the exit.

Little voices started up in my head. What if they knew I'd nicked the roller? What if I didn't roll it properly? What if the fucking thing hasn't worked? What if they're waiting for me? What if? What if?

What if? There was only one way to find out. I clenched my bum cheeks together, gulped air into my mouth, grimaced and walked harmlessly through the alarm system and out onto Oxford Street. In the last rays of the afternoon sunshine, I shook my head in disbelief, strutting along like I'd pulled off the heist of the century, then I came to a juddering halt. Oh shit, Graham I thought, reaching for my radio.

"Charlie seven zero? Charlie seven zero? Charlie seven zero?" he demanded.

"Seven, zero?" I returned.

"At last, seven zero, MK Camden, call me P.O.B. I've got more," he said tersely.

"Roger Rog," I replied letting go of my radio.

Pissing off your controller was about the worst thing you could do as a despatch rider, especially if it was getting near the end of the day. You wanted a job that took you in the same direction as your journey home, then if you were satisfied with your earnings, you could call it a day. Roger, a posh kid from Barnes had got fed up with the 'Roger, Roger, Roger' joke and told Graham to shut up on air. The poor bloke ended up in Birmingham that night before he handed his radio in. Luckily, I'd had a good day, doubled my guarantee in fact, so need not have worried. At 5 o'clock Graham gave me a W1 going Stevenage. Perfect was the word; I couldn't have been happier. I was going to be paid to ride home. Broadcasting House in Portland Place was the pickup. Picking up from the BBC had been a regular occurrence for me over the years and it never ceased to amaze me. Most of the time, there hadn't been anyone on reception and there never seemed to be any security about either. I would wander in, go up to the mail room on the second floor and ask if the pickup was there. It was no different tonight, but when I got to the mail room nobody knew anything about any parcel going anywhere. I checked back with Graham, and he told me I was picking up from DJ Simon Mayo. I thought, great, why can't it be John Peel instead of that wanker Mayonnaise? Twenty minutes and I was still waiting. I thought of calling it in as a cancellation. In fact, I would have done, if the drop hadn't been on my way home. Then, finally, the creamy textured wanker deigned to come into the post room and huffily chucked the package in my direction. The parcel was quite big; it could have been a van job, and again I toyed with the idea of leaving it, or better still telling Mayo to stick it up his self-important little arse crack, but it was going to pay for my ride home. It was time to go. Black Death had performed well on the streets of London, but I couldn't wait to get her out onto the open road. All I needed to do was ride up Portland Place, cut across Regents Park and get on the A1 on the other side of South Hampstead. Then it was the A1 and the open road of the A1M, all the way to Stevenage. I shot off at rocket speed away from Broadcasting House and stopped at the traffic lights on Euston Road. Rush hour traffic blocked my path when the lights turned green, but it was no real problem. I did what I had been doing all day long, wiggled the bulky VFR around the stationary metal work, then sped through the park gate. Immediately, I was doused in blue light. Fucking hell, I thought. Then, seeing it was a Police bike, I thought, oh no, that's fucking worse. Even though both of us loved bikes, the motorcycle cops were always the worst of the boys in blue. It was like we were in opposing biker gangs, the Outlaws and the Hells Angels. Slamming on the anchors, I came to an abrupt halt. Slowly, like he knew I was in a hurry, he slid off his BMW, pressed the button on his radio and relayed something back to his controller. I wanted to say, 'oh come on, I haven't got all fucking night', but looking at this dickhead, that would mean he would take all fucking night.

Eventually, he sidled up, "You know you're not allowed in the Royal Parks, don't you?"

Not only was my first impression correct, he was a proper dickhead, he was wrong too,

"Yes, I am, it's only sign painted vehicles that aren't allowed."

"No, you are not. What's that written on your mail bag?"

"Central Express, but it's not painted on look," I retorted, "And it's not on this side," spinning the bag over, covering the writing.

"No, it's still the same," he said breezily, "Give me your license and MOT."

Unfolding Muttley's bent MOT from this morning, I handed it over with my license.

"OK, yes, OK, very good, very good," he admitted disappointedly.

I snorted, thinking you're supposed to be a biker like me, but you're not. You're just a Tamworth on a BMW. You Bavarian, Motor, Wanker.

"Right then, what about your tax disc?" he said, leaning forward.

Immediately his brow furrowed as he scraped away the mud, then he produced a torch from his tunic pocket to get a better look. "What the?" He mumbled, flipping the switch.

Even from where I was, I could see the Tippex slopped over the original number plate.

"Hmm, no, no this isn't right, where did you get this tax disc from?"

"Look, OK, it was on my other bike," I said thinking quickly, "I swapped it over."

"That's illegal, I'm going to have to …"

Suddenly, he put his hand up and reached for his radio, then he turned his back on me and began pacing up and down.

"Yes, yes, Roger, Roger," he answered sombrely.

"You can go. It's your lucky day, but don't ride in the Royal Parks again, and sort that Tax Disc out," he told me as he got onto his bike.

Bloody hell, that was close I thought. Lucky, lucky, lucky. Leaning forwards, I smeared some more mud on the tax disc and then I got going too. Horrendous was the only word I could use for the traffic, as I knew it would be. But I made it out of London in good time and as soon as I was on the A1M I really opened up the VFR. It felt like it had been kept on a leash all day, but as concrete turned to muddy fields, it flew along, eating up the miles with ease. Soon, I had dropped off at Stevenage, and made my way back to the Farm, hoping for a quiet night. I hadn't thought much about Caitlin or our argument. I was hoping I could go into number 34 without seeing her, but when I stalked in, she was waiting in the kitchen for me. Don't get me wrong, I was still angry with her, but I wasn't in the mood for another row. Not after a day like that. There was nothing else I could do except play this one by ear. I was fucking done in. Caitlin looked at me sourly. I thought, fucking hell, I don't need this and pulled a wane smile.

She burst into tears and sniffed, "I don't know who I am anymore, everything is killing me."

I moved towards her, then stopped, remembering how Aiden had been holding her the night before, "What's the matter?" I asked.

"What's the matter?" She repeated sarcastically, "I'm pregnant. And I'm on my own again," she sobbed, inconsolable now, "I'm pregnant by Den and I should be happy he's gone but I'm not. I don't want to be on my own anymore, Natty needs a dad."

Still, I held back, but I really wanted to comfort her and make her feel better. She didn't deserve this. No one deserved this.

Her head dipped forward; her long dark hair covering her face. "You were right about Den. He's a dodgy bloke. He's a junkie. Not like you. You've got a good heart," she exclaimed, raking her hands through her long dark hair.

"I'm sorry about last night. I wasn't myself last night. I don't know, I won't tell anyone about Kipper. Kipper's a bastard. I hate him."

"Listen, everything's going to be fine. Trust me we'll work it out. You, me, Pete and Natty - we'll be alright. You'll see."

"It won't be, Skinner, I can't be a mother anymore, I'm going insane. My hormones are killing me. I want to kill myself. If it wasn't for Natty I would."

No longer being able to hold back, I gently put my hand under her chin, raised her head up so we were looking into each other's eyes.

"Come on. Don't talk like that; we can work it out," I cooed trying to calm her.

"Listen, it's going to be fine. OK?" I whispered softly.

"Skinner, you're such a nice guy," she breathed back. Then she shut her eyes and came forward to kiss me. I moved to her.

Pete mooched in, "You should see that fucking dog. He's hilarious. He's lying on his back in the sitting room with his feet in the air. He looks like a footstool made of wool," he cackled.

"Pete?!?" I exclaimed.

"Looks like a fucking footstool, man, ha, ha."

"PETE!!?"

"What?" he replied obliviously, grabbing a handful of baby bells out of the fridge.

Caitlin stormed out, her eyes chucking daggers at the stoned idiot.

"Is she going to check out that crazy hound dawg?"

"No, no she's not. Pete, have you any idea what's going on around here?" I asked.

"Nope, and that's why I stay stoned," he said tossing a piece of cheese in the air.

He caught it in his mouth, gave me a lopsided grin. "Stoned is the way of the walk," he gurgled through the masticating cheese, strolling out.

I shook my head,

"Mate, you've changed," I mumbled to an empty room.

 Enough was enough, I needed to rest, get some time on my own to re-charge; re-evaluate. So after a big plate of fish and chips, I went upstairs and put a spliff together myself. Despite what had happened downstairs with Caitlin, there was only one thing on my mind, one thing after a day like that despatch riding. It was always the same. I would scroll back through all the stupid dangerous things I had done, not only putting myself in danger, but other people too. I would always say to myself, that the next day would be different. I would cool down, take it easy, ride safely, but deep down inside I knew, that as soon as I got back on the saddle and the adrenaline kicked in, nothing would change. I would always be searching for that gap in the traffic. Keep the speed up, looking for the red line, and that's how it was for the rest of the week.

ALIENS.

Saturday morning: Stink had decided he wanted to take a stroll around his manor. I knew this because when I came downstairs, he was standing by the front door with my neckerchief in his mouth. And who was I to argue? After all, it was a bright early autumn day. Hitching the little tyke up, I yanked the door open and was immediately hit by a gust of chilly wind. I took a deep breath and filled my lungs, tasted its purity, felt the life affirming sensation as my blood oxygenated, then headed out. Flying in the air around us a whirlwind of colourful leaves bustled, while below they playfully chased each other along the path. Stink, as usual was on point, head down, checking last night's scents, stopping every now and then to add his own view on the mephitic tapestry. Dog shit alley was particularly dangerous today; it was hard to tell where the turds were with all the gyrating leaves, but Stink knew the way, so I followed close behind in his wake. Soon we had got to the play area at the centre of the blocks, and I grabbed his ball from my leather jacket pocket and lobbed it with all my might. Caught by the buffeting wind, the red ball arced high in the air then fell, disappearing in the long brown grass behind the old burned-out roundabout. Stink was off like a rocket. A few minutes later, ball in his grinning mouth, he came pelting out of the grass with another dog chasing close behind him. I creased up laughing. It was another terrier with similar markings to him, only this one was adorned with a pink collar. They could have been from the same litter.

"Who's this? You got yourself a girlfriend have you mate?" I called over at the gallivanting nut job, "Bloody hell you're a fast worker."

Stink came steaming past me with his new friend in close pursuit, then they began to do tight circuits around the rocking horse, yapping excitedly.

"Skinner?" Called out Hippy John, approaching from block six.

"You alright John? I didn't know you had a dog."

"Yeah, I just got her," he told me, his hand feebly flapping at his hair, trying to keep it out of his eyes in the gusting wind. "Is your dog done Skinner?"

"I don't know do I? It's not really my dog, it's Basher's. Stinky Terrier, isn't it? You remember him?"

Hippy John squinted. "Oh yeah, Hillsey was looking after him, wasn't he?"

"Hillsey?" I snapped trying to suppress the image forming in my mind. Too late: *"Your furry friends love it! Especially the rich brown sauce..."* Aaaaaaahhh, fuck off.

Hippy John gave me a puzzled look, then shrugged. "Mine's not done either," he said, watching them belting back into the long grass.

Blasts of wind rippled the rough grass while we waited for them to reappear. Hippy John and me exchanged a glance and then they both came pegging it back towards us.

Hippy John grinned. "Fuck, that was quick."

"Nah, they didn't do anything. If your dog gets up the duff, it's nothing to do with us is it boy? Is it boy?" I told him, leaning over to ruffle his neckerchief.

Stink looked up, tongue lolling, pupils like pin pricks scrutinising me with that great expectation he always did on a walk. He was a funny little thing. He always looked like he'd had the time of his life, the best time he'd ever had, whatever we had been up to. Whether he'd jumped his female counterpart I didn't know. When it came down to it, I couldn't have cared less. If he was happy and he certainly looked it. That was the most important thing.

"We'll see... Or I'll see anyway," laughed Hippy John, "I'm off up to Grantchester Meadows tomorrow morning for the last of the shroomies, you up for that?"

"Am I? Yeah of course mate."

Hippy John nodded sagely, "Thought so, I'll see you tomorrow, Skinner, come on Trudy, come on," he said, and they waddled back towards their block.

"You too, come on Stink, let's go," I said threading the green twine around his neckerchief.

Needing to think a few things through, I decided to take the long way back. Inside the protective cover of the trees at the south of the Farm it would be an easier walk too. Caitlin was on my mind again. On Monday night when I came in from work, I'd found her alone, curled up crying her heart out on the settee in the living room. She told me she'd lost her baby; the poor thing was absolutely devastated. To start with, I didn't know what to say, then slowly but surely, I began to find the words she needed to hear. I felt grown up, like I was taking responsibility for someone else's well-being. It felt good to be making a difference and even better when she started smiling again. What an infectious smile it was too. Caitlin was thirty, almost ten years older than me and being Den's girlfriend, I'd never thought of her as anything else, but something changed that night. Between us a barrier shifted and fell away; we found a connection, a connection I had never had with anyone else before. Cerys and me had been two kids growing up together on a voyage of discovery; we were just growing into ourselves. Mia and me were two versions of the same people, again just finding out who we were, but with Caitlin it was different. She was confident, had lived a life, seen plenty, ups and downs, she knew who she was and was happy in her own skin. Even though I'd felt sorry for her losing her baby, as the week had gone by, the pity I felt ebbed away and I began to enjoy her company. Not just as a friend either. Sexually, nothing had happened between us, but we'd talked a lot and shared a couple of cuddles together on the settee. Sighing to myself like a lovesick puppy, I turned onto the field where I'd met Ridsey's little brother Ed Ridley and his mates. If that little cheese-dick Ed and his poncy mates are about, I thought they'll get one warning. Then if they carry on talking shit, there will be nothing else for it. It would be 'sic 'em boy'! Stink barked appreciatively as the wind propelled us through the washing lines in the yard towards the navy-blue door of number 34. Cracking a grin at the little wire wool mind reader I thought, yes mate, one hundred per cent. Although the wind had been bracing to start with, woke me up, set me up, now I was feeling the creeping fingers of cold inside my leather jacket. It was time to get inside, time for a warm-up. Stink nosed his way through the front door as usual and straight away I felt the warm embrace of the flat. Tea would be good, I thought. Then I'll give Renny a bell, see if there's any gigs on tonight and tell him about Hippy John's plans for tomorrow morning. Stink trotted into the kitchen to his water bowl and got stuck in, while I hung up his accessories in the hall, grinning at the noise the nutter made lapping.

Natty came crashing downstairs, her smile like sunshine. Ignoring me, she went to greet him, "Stinky, Stink," she sang, "Stinky Stink."

"Hi Natty," I called out.

"Stinky doggy, Stinky doggy," she sang, skipping around the pine table.

"Hello? Am I the invisible man now?"

Natty stopped and looked down, "No."

"Oh, right. OK," I returned, surprised by her lack of interest in me. I tried again, "Do you want to play guitar now? There's time before lunch?"

"Don't want to."

"Maybe later then," I said disappointedly watching her skip out, taking the sun with her.

My hands were so cold, I doubt I would have been able to play much anyway, so I put the kettle on, rubbing some warmth into them.

From the living room there was a laugh, then voices, bloke's voices.

"Does anyone want a cup of tea?" I called out.

"Yeah, go on then, why not? Make it a baaaad ass one, ink with four sugars."

It sounded like Aiden.

Oh no, not that knob end, I thought and went to investigate. It was that knob end. He lolled back puffing a roll up in Pete's chair with Natty sitting on his knee giggling up at him.

Den was lounging on the settee with Caitlin, his arm draped protectively over her shoulder. Both Den and Aiden had that sweaty smackhead complexion. Everything I'd been hearing from Renny looked to be true.

"Skinner, long time no see, been out with our new dog?" enquired Den, cordially enough.

My eyes went from Den to Caitlin, then back to Den.

"Cat got your tongue Skinner?" Asked Aiden, a silly grin bisecting his face.

"Dog got his tongue, more like," corrected Den, sending Natty into fits of laughter.

My eyes bored into Caitlin, "Yeah, something like that."

Caitlin held my stare.

"I need to make a call, kettle's just boiled," I said pulling a tight smile.

Den put his palm up, "Skinner, me and Caitlin have got some news haven't we darling?" He smiled cupping his other hand over her belly, "Caitlin's pregnant, I'm going to be a dad."

Cracking a smile, she put her hand onto his and gave it a squeeze.

"Nice one. Congratulations," I spat in her direction.

Caitlin still held my stare and said nothing, what she was expecting me to say I didn't know, she just stroked Den's grubby hand holding their baby. Confusion, anger and not just a little bit of hurt surged through me. There was only one thing on my mind at that moment. Get out of here, get out fast. Time to fuck off and lick my wounds before they turned septic. Explanations would have to wait; I didn't know who knew what, but Caitlin knowing what a fucking mug I'd been was humiliation enough. How things could change? Only seconds earlier, it was a nice cup of tea and a warm-up. Now I couldn't wait to get back out in the biting wind, but a walk around the block wouldn't be enough. I needed to get away. Get away for a while.

Picking up the phone I dialled Mia's number, "Hi Mia, how's it going?" I asked, hearing her sweet voice.

"Hiya Skinner," she replied breezily, "I'm good thanks, it's a long time since I've heard from you. Are you still freezing your bollocks off biking?"

Clearly, she was happy to hear my voice too.

"Yeah," I chuckled, "I've got ice cubes for bollocks now."

Mia laughed. "Awww, haven't you got anyone to warm them up for you?"

"Yeah, they're queuing up around the block," I returned.

Mia giggled back, "I bet they are too."

"Listen Mia, I need to get away from here," I said pulling the receiver in close, "Can I come up yours tonight, maybe stop over?"

"Tonight?"

"Yeah, if that's OK? I'm meeting some mates in Grantchester tomorrow. We're getting some shrooms, you can come to. What do you reckon?"

"That's short notice," she said, thinking, "No, no. I'm busy tonight, Skinner, tomorrow too."

"Oh what, really? You don't fancy shroomies with a view?"

Mia snorted, "No, no, you can't just phone me up and expect me to drop everything. Sorry I'm busy. I've got a life too you know?"

"Alright, but if you change your mind… shrooomies?!?"

Mia sighed, "I'm not going to change my mind. I'm busy. Sodding hell Skinner, you don't half push it sometimes."

"OK, OK, yeah sorry Mia, I should have known better, I just needed to get out of dodge for a couple of days."

"Oh Skinner, don't worry about it, it's fine. There're a few cowboys around here I'd like to get away from too… Look, I've got to go now, I'll give you a bell next week, OK? See you. Oh, and have a good trip," she said and hung up.

Simply put, I'd made a prat of myself; what I was thinking, I don't know. Mia always had plans for the weekend, she had a huge network of friends to keep up with. I would have been put out myself if someone had phoned me, expecting me to drop everything for them. Not with Mia though, dropping everything for her came naturally to most blokes as she possessed the unique combination of intelligence and rebelliousness. I was lucky she spent any time with me at all. She was well out of my league. Putting the receiver down I scratched at my stubble, thinking, Renny was in, so that's where I was heading. Without saying goodbye, I marched out of the flat into the buffeting wind. A few windswept minutes later I impatiently rapped on his door, hoping his Nan Nora wouldn't answer. She'd steadily been getting worse and worse.

The door cracked open; a voice hissed. "Have you come for the secret documents?"

Oh, shit I thought, here we go again.

"Hello?" Nora? I've come to see Renny," I said raising my voice.

"Shhhhh, they'll hear you."

"Renny?" I shouted up at the open upstairs window.

"Be quiet. Careless talk costs lives."

"Renny, I know you're up there man, I can hear you laughing. Come on, it's not funny, let me in, please man."

"Shut up, you fool. You'll get us all caught."

"Rennnnyyyy!!?"

"Calm yourself young Skinner," said Renny, appearing in the porch.

"Come on you silly old thing. It's not the Gestapo. It's only Skinner, he's harmless, well most of the time anyway," he chided

Renny, gently took her arm and guided her back into the house.

"You're going to the day centre with Hippy John's mum, you remember?"

"Hippies? I don't like blinking hippies. Conscientious objectors. Bunch of 5th columnists the lot of them," she told him, "Where were they when we needed them? Wearing their wives bloomers, and hiding in the blinking coal shed, that's where."

"Yeah, that's right Nan, long haired bloody Yetis," he winked at me.

"Come on Nan, I've got your handbag here, they'll be playing bingo today, won't they?"

"Ooh yes bingo. I love the bingo," she smiled, looking off into the distance. "BINGO!!" She called out excitedly, her face lighting up.

Renny smiled indulgently, "Yeah, that's it. Bingo!!" he repeated, "And you make sure you win me something for me this time won't you?" He laughed. Then, looking at me over his shoulder, he said, "Go sit in the living room and I'll be there in a minute or two."

Nodding my head I said, "OK mate, you be alright?"

"Yeah, she's alright, I'll sort her out. See you in a minute."

In the middle of the living room on an occasional table sat a box. Straight away I recognised it as one of Robbo's bootleg VHS boxes, so I ripped open the top and had a look inside. *Aliens* sat on the top of the pile. Underneath, *Platoon* and *Predator* glistened back invitingly in their plastic covers. That's this afternoon sorted I thought.

"Sorry about that Skinner, the old girl's not all there these days. I don't know if I told you but last week, she was out in the garden at one in the morning calling my grandad in for his tea." He had told me alright. He'd summed it up by saying, 'Nora's gone batty', paraphrasing Nora Batty off, 'The last of the summer wine,' but he was off his nut at the time. He sat down on the settee, ran his tattooed hand back through his short black spiked hair,

"Bad news Skinner, I tell you, I don't know what she's going to do next. I can't be around here all the time; I've got to earn. I've got to earn for both of us. Her pension's fucking shit."

Renny had never really opened up to me about his Nan before, and the truth was I didn't know what to say, so I nodded and let him carry on.

"People don't understand, they keep saying I should put her in a home. But it would break her heart to leave my grandad's garden, she loves it out there in the summer."

"Well, you can't do that then, can you mate?"

"No, no way. Fuck them," he declared, shaking his head, "I'm all she's got now. I'm not going to let her down. She's a pain in the arse, but she's alright really."

Exhaling deeply, I thought yeah well, that just about sums parents up.

"I suppose that's the way it is, with life and all that," he carried on, "They look after us when we're kids and then if we're good people we look after them when they need us later on."

"Yeah, well my parents don't need looking after, they live in Cornwall."

Renny snorted, shaking his head, "What are you going on about? Fucking Skinner."

Grinning, I put my palms up.

He sighed. "Man, you are so shallow," he cackled, "Bird bath shallow," he concluded.

I cracked up laughing, "Not even that mate, robins and blackbirds would bump their heads."

Then both of us were laughing.

"What we doing then?" I asked, eyeing the box of VHS tapes on the table between us.

Renny pulled out a big fat Thai stick from his top pocket, "Fuck the whole world for today. How's that sound Skinner?"

The way I was feeling, I couldn't have agreed more.

"In which order?" he asked, fanning the three blockbusters out in his hands like giant playing cards.

"Er... what about comedy, action, then deep space to finish with?"

"You want *Platoon* first?" He laughed.

Laughing back, I said, "No, *Predator* first, *Platoon* then *Aliens*, yeah?"

"Right you are – makes sense," he agreed, ramming the *Predator* vid home into the bulky VHS player, then he pressed down hard on the play button, and we waited.

Renny and me sat back puffing the afternoon away watching Arnie destroy the dreadlock predator, Oliver Stone's character endure the horror of Vietnam, then finally Ripley's struggle against the giant insect like beings in Aliens. Once we'd finished, we went up the chippy on Windsor Drive, got some grub and then when we returned, the mammoth VHS/Thai stick session continued. Sergio Leone's spaghetti western T*he Good, the Bad and the Ugly* with Tuco, Angel Eyes, and the man with no name was up next. Only once had I watched the film all the way through. That was with my old man. Every other time I had fallen asleep, and it was no different this time. As the brilliant and epic meandering story slowly weaved its way across the silver screen, I soon nodded off. I'm not sure how long I was asleep for but when I woke up, the TV was off, as was the lamp on the occasional table. The only light in the room was the orange-tinged light coming around the curtain from the streetlights. Blinking a couple of times while my eyes got accustomed to the fragile light, I stretched my arms out crucifix like, then looked over at the settee. Renny must have gone to bed, but there was no way I was going home, so I hauled myself over, dropped down onto it and got comfortable. My thoughts began to race. No, no fucking way was I going back there tonight. I needed more time, a lot more time. More time to let the bile rescind, to let the hurt go, and most importantly time to formulate some kind of plan of action. The bullshit Caitlin had pulled on me couldn't be left unanswered. My self-respect was in tatters. In amongst the tropical islands, the paddy fields of Vietnam and far off galaxies, I hadn't thought about it much, but somehow, I had digested it, and it seemed a lot clearer now. I had been a complete mug, a dozy twat there for the taking. Still, I didn't know whether Caitlin had lost her baby or not, but my belief was she was still pregnant, and she'd lied to me to get my sympathy. Fuck knows what she would have said if we'd have got together as a couple. She'd have probably told me the baby was mine and like the fucking mug I was, I would have believed her. It was like Caitlin was some kind of twisted version of Ripley in the Aliens movie, but instead of trying to rid herself of the Alien's spawn, she was keeping it quiet, keeping it safe while it gestated. Nine months later, Den's baby would have been born, and I'd have been none the wiser. Then later when I found out; and I would have found out, because these things always find a way. That's when the tearing of the flesh would have begun. My heart would have been ripped into little pieces. No. No way could this go unanswered, was my last thought before I drifted off into a fitful sleep…

> Incredible was the only way I could describe the heat; My body roasted inside the confines of my skintight space suit. Sweat ran down my forehead into my tired eyes; out of habit my hand reached up to clear it away, but it brushed off the plexiglass visor of my space helmet. My vision was distorted but I could still make out dozens of dark foreboding mounds all around me. Throwing my ungainly space boot forward in the light atmosphere I kicked into something solid. I felt myself going over, so I threw a glove onto one of the mounds. Deep within something moved; my hand shot upwards like I'd been electrocuted. Dull pulses of yellow green light rippled across its rough surface. Then it split open at the top emitting a loud hiss. Every bone in my body told me to back off. Run. Get back to the spaceship. But I was intrigued. Enthralled. Slowly, I leant forward over the gaping hole and looked into the darkness. From out of the gloom Den's face appeared. Then it shot upwards, smashing my plexiglass visor, throwing me backwards. My gloved hands flailed uselessly. My eyes began to burn. My throat constricted. Then something began lashing at my legs.

"Aaaaaahhh. Jesus Christ? What's going on?" I shouted waking up.

My eyes blinked open to see a walking stick raining down on my thighs.

"What the fucking hell?" I said, blinking furiously.

"Who are you?" Screamed Nora, Renny's Nan, keeping up the pounding.

"Skinner, Skinner. It's me Skinner!!"

"I don't know any Skimmers, who are you? What are you doing in my house? After my purse I bet," she scoffed, going for my head.

"Ouww, Jesus Christ, stop! Renny?" I pleaded putting my arms up.

"Rennie?" She screamed, swinging right to get around my defence.

"Renny, yes, Renny."

"She's been dead for fifteen years."

"She?"

"Yes, she? My daughter Rennie's been dead for seventeen years this November, seventeen years. Not that you'd care," she raged, finding a way around my defence.

"RENNY. RENNY, RENNNYYY. WAKE UP FOR FUCKS... Aarrrhh get off!" I cried, trying to hold her off.

"I'm phoning the police. You'd better stay put. If you move a muscle, I'll give you a four penny one, and no mistake."

Renny flew into the room and grabbed her from behind. Her eyes widened in terror, then she began screaming,

"Aaaaaaaaahhhhh, help police, police, helllp me someone, please, someone, heeelpp me."

"Nan? Nan? Naaannn. Calm down for god's sake," he told her, spinning her around, making eye contact.

"Renny? ...Renny," she realised.

"Yes, Nan - it's me Nan."

The stick fell from her hand, "Oh my... Oh I was, I'm, oh."

"Come on Nan, it's OK now. It's all over now, come on settle down. I'll make you a nice cup of tea," he cooed, gently taking her arm.

"But what about him?" She raged pointing an accusing finger at me, "He said your mum was still alive. He's a liar, the cancer took her. I watched her die. It took three months."

"Nan, believe me, he's not. It's only Skinner; he's my friend, he stopped over, I did tell you but... Oh, don't worry about it. Look, come on, let's get you some breakfast then you can sit in the garden window, come on. It's alright."

She uttered, "I'm sorry Renny," as he led her out.

Sighing, I eased back onto the settee, rubbing my aching thigh, thinking about that old Chinese proverb. 'If everyone in the world brought their troubles to a table, they'd be glad to take theirs back with them'. Certainly, that was true this morning. The poor old girl. She was all over the place, didn't know what was what. Poor Renny too. Sure, I had problems, but they were nothing compared to his. I had choices. My problems could be solved by moving out or better still getting them moved out, but that wasn't an option for Renny. What was he supposed to do? He couldn't put her in a home, he was too loyal, so that was it. He had no choice. A bit of morality and a bit of loyalty meant, he was backed into a corner.

"It's OK Skinner, it's safe to come out now," said Renny pulling a tired grin, coming back into the room with a tray of tea and toast.

"I didn't do anything mate, I promise you."

"Don't worry about it, I know you didn't, she's barking fucking mad these days, sometimes she doesn't even know who I am."

"Nora's batty," I concluded snatching a piece of toast.

Renny paused, scrutinising me,

"That's one of mine, isn't it?" he asked.

I replied, "Yeah, sorry man," and shut my stupid mouth.

"No don't worry about it. If you can't laugh about the shit going on in the world, what are you going to do? it's a cold fucking world mate."

"Yeah, that's right, Renny."

"Bet that fucking freaked you out her coming in battering you?" He grinned picking up his teacup and warming his hands, keen to move on.

"Fucking, did it? I was dreaming about that *Aliens* film; I thought I was being attacked by one of those face sucking egg things."

Renny nearly choked on his tea, "I bet."

"It could have been so different, I could have been banging Mia in her bed, but instead I slept on your settee and got woken up getting banged by your Nan," I said, smiling.

Renny creased up laughing, then grabbed a piece of toast, waiting for me to tell him more, so I did. When I finished, he shook his head.

"You phoned up Mia on a Saturday and wanted her to drop everything for you?"

I sniggered lecherously, "She always drops everything for me."

"Ha, ha, yeah good one."

"I was hoping I'd meet you lot up in Grantchester today, I invited her along too."

Renny snorted, "I bet that went down like a Led Zeppelin, fucking hell Skinner, what's up with you mate? You can't do that to a girl like Mia, she's a rocker, she's always out. I'm surprised she didn't tell you to fuck off."

Now it was my turn to snort, "She wouldn't do that," I said, thinking, did she?

"Mia and me see each other now and again, she's sound mate, she told me to give her a call, so no harm done."

As soon as it was out of my mouth, I regretted it.

"Oh no, not the old don't call us we'll call you, the cheque's in the post thing again is it? I told you about that with Cerys, remember?"

"Yeah, I remember," I groaned, knowing what was coming.

"Well, has she called you yet? It must be what three, four years now," he laughed, putting his empty tea cup down and reaching for his roll ups.

"Yeah, yeah, yeah, ha de ha, go on laugh it up."

Renny knew Cerys had come to the hospital to see me after the crash and how upset she had been about it. He also knew that she'd signed up as a nurse on a Mediterranean cruise ship a couple of months afterwards.

"OK Casanova, leave it out. How's Carrie these days," I threw back.

"Don't know, don't care. You remember her mate, Alice? That goth girl? The one who wanted to meet you?"

"Yeah?" I said warily, half-knowing what was coming.

"I'm seeing her now," he told me conclusively, standing up, "Right, I'll just check on Nan and see she's OK. Then we better get going. Hippy John reckoned he'd be here at half six."

Renny disappeared upstairs while I demolished the rest of the tea and toast. Soon, we were standing outside his house on Windsor Drive. The gale seemed to have blown itself out, but it was still freezing cold, so I wrapped my leather jacket around me, trying to seal up any gaps.

"Where is the stupid fucking hippy?" I moaned, shivering.

Then, just like I had summoned him up from some kind of psychedelic never, never world, his light blue Commer camper van appeared out of the mist on Thieves Lane.

"Ta, dah," said a grinning Renny.

Breathing a frosty sigh of relief, I started thinking about the heater and how I was going to bogey it, but then from somewhere deep inside me, alarm bells began to ring,

"No, oh no, please no. Is that PJ sitting in the back?"

"Yeah, Hippy John reckons he knows where all the best mushy spots are. He used to do shrooms with Syd Barret."

"Sure, he did!! Was it two weeks before he met Mickie Most? Maybe a week after he swam the channel on acid? Or was it a day after the Nuremberg trials?"

Hippy John pulled up next to us, grinning through the grimy window.

"Probably," he said, "Come on Skinner. In you get."

BYRON'S POOL.

Hippy John's Commer Camper van must have been the slowest vehicle in the world. It had no pull away and no top end. Inside it was noisy too, it had no bonnet which meant the clapped-out old engine sat directly underneath us. After a fitful night and a rude awakening by the Alien's Nan early that morning, I was hoping to get a bit of sleep on the way to Grantchester, but it was impossible. Every time Hippy John lifted his foot off the accelerator, the engine backfired. It wasn't just a few little pop-pops either. If he lifted his foot off quickly, the backfires sounded like a shotgun being fired. PJ didn't seem too bothered by it though. He was totally sparko. He was like a fucking rag doll; he was completely in tune with the van's movements. His head rocked backwards when it accelerated, lolled forward when it decelerated and when Hippy John spun the wheel right to take a corner, PJ's head would flop onto my shoulder. It was well out of order. I had to keep pushing him away before he dribbled on my leather jacket. Renny offered me a wake and bake smoke as we struggled up Ware hill in second gear on the approach to Thundridge, my old village. Nodding like PJ, I took the Thai stick laced spliff that he'd been sharing with Hippy John in the front. Wake and bake wasn't normally my thing. Usually, I'd like to get something done before having a smoke, but this morning I just didn't give a fuck. I still felt wronged by Caitlin. I had been totally out manoeuvred by her. Then bulldozed and paved over. I felt like a proper twat.

"You two love birds alright in the back there?" Called out Renny over the rasping noise of the clapped-out engine.

Propelling PJ's hairy lolling bonce off my shoulder I said, "Yeah, I'm alright. I had a bit of aggro with Caitlin yesterday."

"What?" He exclaimed.

"I had a bit of trouble with Caitlin yesterday."

His head spun around, "Caitlin? Trouble? You never said? Oooohhh. You're not fucking messing with her, are you?"

"Nah, not really," I told them, already regretting starting the conversation.

"Keep clear of that Skinner, she's a nutter. She used to go around with Paige Stamp."

Blowing out a geyser of smoke, I passed the spliff back to him and turned to the window as we crested the steep hill.

Hippy John said, "He's right Skinner, the blokes she's been with are psychos, proper bad men, most of them have done time."

I bit at my fingernail, then aware of doing it, I stopped.

Hippy John's eyes scanned me from the rear-view mirror, "Tell you what though, her little kid Natalie has turned out alright, hasn't she?" he told me, brightening, "Considering who she is, she's amazing man, a good little guitarist too."

"Yeah," I smiled, feeling proud.

"Who would have thought Aiden would be such a good teacher?"

"What? Aiden? Nah It's me. I'm teaching her."

Renny swivelled in his seat again. Hippy John's eyes sought me out again, "Really? Caitlin told me it was Aiden."

"No, it's me. For fucks sake. Don't believe anything that conniving bitch says."

Renny grimaced, looked to Hippy John, "Oh, nooo, he has been fucking messing with her, hasn't he?"

"Fucking with her? Or messing with her?"

"Both are dangerous."

Hippy John exhaled, "Indeed, they are. Ohhh Skinner, tsk,tsk."

"Hardy-Ha. Smart. And both of you can piss off," I said, as we slowly trundled passed the Thundridge village sign.

Renny and Hippy John's conversation continued. Not that I could hear it, because it was lost in the racket of the stuttering engine.

Taking a moment, I disappeared inside myself while watching the familiar sights of the village, scrolling past the window. Den had done me a favour coming back. A fucking big one. Because of his return, I wouldn't have to bring his kid up not knowing it wasn't mine, and although I would never call Natty baggage, who knew what else Caitlin was carrying around. In the end, if something bad happened to me, I would always try to find some kind of good in it. Sometimes, it was the only way to survive.

"Earth calling Skinner, Earth calling Skinner... Do you read me?" Called Renny. "You used to live around here, didn't you?"

"Yeah, most of my life man."

Hippy John pointed to a slim peroxide blonde girl in her mid-twenties walking past the Feathers Pub, "Whoa, who is that? She's well horny, is that an old girlfriend of yours?"

Narrowing my eyes in the glare of the misty morning sunshine, I recognised Hayley Williams, Dave's older sister.

I smiled, "Hmm not quite. I was close, but no cigar mate."

"No cigar," repeated Hippy John, belly laughing.

"You remember that band I was in, VirusV1? Thats the drummer's sister, Hayley."

"Dave Williams was the drummer in Virus V1, formed in 1979, broke up in 1983," intoned Renny, showing off his complete knowledge of punk bands.

I wound my window down. "Here pull over, let's say hello."

Hippy John slammed on the brakes.

B.BAAAANNNGGG went the engine.

Hayley visibly jumped, then gaped at the strangers ogling her from the old dilapidated camper van.

"Hayley? You alright?"

Even as a kid her eyesight wasn't the best, but it must have deteriorated further because she didn't know who we were. She just stood squinting, mole-like.

Renny grinned, "No wonder she liked you Skinner. She's as blind as a bat."

"Fuck man, her eyesight was fine back then... Well, maybe not," I conceded, cracking up.

"Come on let's go," I said winding the window up, "She doesn't recognise me."

"She doesn't want to, more like," retorted Renny, back on the wind up.

"Yeah, yeah, yeah good one," I chuckled.

"Blind or not, that Hayley is horny, well horny, I'd crawl through dog shit laced glass just to sniff her pantyhose," said Hippy John haltingly pulling away.

I snorted, "Yeah, well if I see her, I'll pass that along … Perv."

On the way up the daunting High Cross Hill, the van struggled so much that I thought, Renny, PJ and me, would have to get out to lighten the load, but Hippy John knew it's limitations all too well. He about turned and reversed the camper van up the steep incline. I'll give it its due, it made it to the top, even though it was at a speed of 9 MPH. Not long after we'd negotiated the obstacle of the Rib valley, we drove out onto the rolling hills of Hertfordshire. Colliers End, Puckeridge, and Buntingford all disappeared in folds of green countryside. Then when we got into Royston, a tight corner had PJ's rolling head bounce off the window.

He stirred, "Hey Donovan man, is this the right pea green?" he murmured, almost inaudibly shaking his thinning grey hair. Then back on a planet near earth, his head rose up and he said,

"Hi Skinner, I was having this amazing dream, man."

"Oh yeah?" I replied tentatively, thinking, here we fucking go.

"Yeah man, I was an owl and Donovan was a pussycat, it was stargazy. Out of this world man. We set sail in a pea green boat and travelled to a place where the bong tree grows."

"Bong tree," I laughed, "Sounds good PJ."

Renny saw the look on my face and egged him on, "You used to know that Donovan dude, the mellow yellow man, didn't you PJ?"

PJ straightened up, pulled a rubber band from his pocket, then threaded his unkempt salt and pepper hair through it, "I knew Donnie very well, I met him two weeks after I swam naked in the Turpentine with Princess Margaret, a year after I smoked opium with Lulu, three months before Ronnie Kray introduced me to Barbara Windsor..."

My hands rose up to meet my face, but before burying myself, I noticed Renny burst out laughing. He was having a great time. He was alright, he couldn't hear much over the thumping engine. I could though, it was right in my ear hole.

PJ was in full on tripped out hippy flow. It was an endless, exhausting hit parade of sixties' faces name dropping. "If memory serves me correctly it was two years before I met Brit Ekland through Rod the mod, and six months before I caught syphilis off Christine Keeler…"

On and on he went then I thought fuck this, why am I listening to this? This is bullshit. Let's take a leaf out of my old man's book and challenge him, that'll shut him up.

"Whoa, hold on hold on, OK so what happened with you and Christine Keeler?"

PJ looked totally taken a back, then he thought about it. Finally, he said, "I can't remember."

"It was the sixties Skinner," chipped in Hippy John.

I ignored him, "What happened when you met poxy, 'Donnie' then?"

Again, PJ paused, visibly straining, like he was taking a shit, trying to push the memory out, then he smiled and said, "I don't want to remember."

"You don't want to remember?"

"Yes, because that's what life is all about Skinner. The highlights. When you get older the highlights are the only things that matter."

"What? What does that mean?"

"In a few years' time, highlights will be the only things people will be interested in. It's already happening in the USA; people's attention span is minuscule."

"Nah, come on, everyone likes a story, don't they?"

"They do, but their limited capacity won't be able to digest it."

PJ leant in and whispered, "And also Skinner, the devil is in the details, and nobody wants the devil."

"That's just a stupid saying."

"Is it? Is it, my friend?" He said with a self-satisfied smile, and with that, he placed his arms at his side and looked off into the distance.

Hippy John and Renny were in stitches.

"Renny?" I called out.

"What?" He said turning, his eyes wet from laughing.

"Are we nearly there yet?"

"Nope. There's about twenty miles to go," he said, laughing some more.

"Oh, come on Renny don't please. I'd chuck myself out of the window and end it all now if I could, but we're going too slow."

Renny creased up, "I'm telling you, there's about twenty miles to go... or is it thirty?"

"Don't listen to him Skinner," said Hippy John, "It's only a few more minutes."

"Thank fuck for that," I mumbled into the din of the engine.

Hippy John drove the irksome camper van over the M11, then turned right at the first roundabout, which brought us into Grantchester. It was like we'd gone back in time, driven into a John Constable painting. At any moment I expected to hear the clip-clop of horse's hooves on the cobblestones, but there was nothing, there was nobody around. Good news for us I thought, the less people about the better. We could pick a tea pot full of shrooms and get back to Lenny's by, well, judging by how long it had taken us to get here, by this evening. Hippy John took a right at the T-junction at the centre of the village as PJ had directed. Then we passed an old pub and some even older thatched houses, one of them being a huge vicarage.

"We are nearly there now Skinner," PJ informed me smiling happily, "Just follow the road around to the right John, then after we cross the bridge, start looking for somewhere to stop."

Hippy John nodded slowly as he coaxed the hapless vehicle into the tight bend.

"That's the River Cam, isn't it?"

"Yes, it is, and there is Byron's Pool," PJ told us, with not just a little bit of pride in his voice,

"Do you know of Lord Byron Skinner?"

"Yeah of course."

"Hmmm," he murmured doubtfully, but it was true. I knew quite a bit about him as Doggy was a massive fan of his. He had found solace in Lord Byron's work while he struggled against his parent's wishes for him to read business at Cambridge University.

Enthralled now in its gleaming surface, I asked, "You into him then?"

PJ chuckled, "Didn't you know? I'm related to him."

"Bollocks, come on?"

"Yes, it is true," he said sticking his white stubbly chin out.

Two things came to mind: one, he was talking bullshit, and two: even though he was talking bullshit, we were actually having a two-way conversation.

"It's true Skinner," Hippy John chimed in, "He's a descendant of one of his cousins, I've seen his family tree."

"Are you mad, bad and dangerous to know, PJ?" I quoted Lady Caroline Lamb's description of him.

"I've had my moments over the years."

Renny snorted, "Mad, bad and fucking boring to know, more like. Come on pull over here, this will do. Let's get the shroomies."

Hippy John steered onto the grass verge and rolled to a stop in front of an old rotting five bar gate. Free at last, I jumped out, yawned expansively and was about to stretch my aching legs, when a muddy Land Rover skidded to a halt at the back of the van.

The window wound down to reveal a ruddy faced farmer, "Oi wouldn't park there if oi was you, you're blocking that gate, son. Oi don't mind, but if my faather comes down, he'll knock that van out of the way with his tractorrr. You see, he's not loike me," he called over.

"Yeah, OK mate no problem," I told him evenly, giving him the thumbs up and hopped back in the van.

"What's going on?" Demanded Renny.

"Farmer bloke reckons we can't park here," I told him.

"Oh yeah? What did he say?"

"Nothing mate, he was on the wind up, he reckons his old man was going to ram our van out of the way," I laughed.

"Is that fucking right?" He snarled, throwing the door open.

"Come on, it's not worth it," implored Hippy John, starting the engine.

"Wait here," Renny told him in no uncertain terms, but by the time he got around the back of the van the farmer had driven off.

Renny stomped out into the road, spying the retreating vehicle. "Yeah, you better drive off. Go on fuck off you inbred wanker."

A few moments later he climbed back into the van. "Why didn't you hit him, Skinner?"

"What? Nah, I'm not going to do that, am I?"

"He was having a go."

"He didn't bother me," I returned evenly.

Hippy John sighed, putting the van into gear, "Come on, can we leave it? Let's go back to the field near the pool, yeah?"

Renny exhaled, "If anyone talked to me like that, I'd at least have said something back."

Exhaling, I rolled my eyes and sat back as the Commer bumped back onto the road.

"Skinner's right Renny," said Hippy John huffily, "It wasn't worth it, an eye for an eye makes the whole world blind."

"Er, no, nobody took my eye mate, it was fine."

Renny ignored me and whacked his hand on the dashboard, "Listen. If someone takes my eye and I take his back, then he'll think twice about taking my other one."

PJ leant towards Renny, "My friend, one ounce of patience is worth a ton of preaching."

"Fucks sake, I'm in a van with the Gandhi twins."

Hippy John grinned, spun the huge steering wheel to the left and we turned off the main road and onto a sweeping track that led us towards the gleaming pool.

On the way up Hippy John had told us Commer's weren't made for off roading, and he was right. Fucking hell, was he? It was a bone-shaking, ass hurting, head nodding ride, until eventually, we made it into an oblong-shaped meadow next to the pool.

"There it is. The pool of my ancestors," PJ drooled, ingesting it.

"Man, that is amazing. It looks like a mirror," I enthused.

"It does Skinner. It's a mirror of life," concurred PJ clambering out onto the solid grass,

"Ouch... I've got a bit of a club foot... Byron had one, you know?"

"Did he? Wow," I answered absently, taking in our surroundings.

On one side of Byron's Pool, there was a small footbridge that crossed over a weir, which let fresh water in from the River Cam.

To the other side, large trees rose up triumphantly, projecting their fiery reds and oranges onto the still waters.

Renny sidled up to me, "Shit a brick. Not you as well?" He nodded towards the other two who were taking it in as well, "You'll be like them soon," he stated.

"Renny, leave it out man, it's beautiful. What do you see?"

"A pond?"

I snorted, "How about over there?" I said pointing down field.

"A field?"

"Bollocks, come on, you've got to see that. PJ says the devil is in the details, but there's good in the details too... That's the details," I kept on, pointing at the boundary of trees with their autumn tints of reds, yellows and oranges.

"Yeah, I suppose, it's alright," he almost conceded.

Oh well, that's a start, I thought. Leaving him to his one-dimensional world, I continued to take the beauty in. Behind the fired boundary, the sun shone. Soft rays of light glided through the foliage, highlighting the white powdery frost under our feet.

"Oh what, no fucking way."

"What's up Hippy Skinner?" laughed Renny.

"I'll tell you what's up. It's frosty," I cried.

"Yeah, far out Skinner," he said, still trying to take the piss.

"Shut up, you dickhead."

That got everyone's attention. Nobody said that to Renny.

"Frost kills off mushroom spores, there'll be fuck all here."

Renny eyed the two Johns, "Is that true?"

"No, of course not," blustered PJ, "I've been picking magic mushrooms on Grantchester Meadows for thirty years."

"You missed the devil in the details!" I crowed.

"What's this devil? What details?"

"The details that the first frost is the end of the mushroom season. Those fucking details."

"Huh? Calm yourself dear fellow and follow me," PJ said adamantly, fanning his arms out to indicate that we should spread out, "There'll be plenty, plenty for all, you'll see."

Kicking through the long powdery grass, we did a couple of futile sweeps around the van.

"Ah," said PJ magnanimously, stooping low, "Here we are!"

Renny smirked at me, "What you got PJ?"

PJ smiled at me ingratiatingly, "Here you are, ye of little faith, no devils here," opening his hand to reveal six white caps.

"Brilliant, that's what, one and a half each?"

"Not even that," chuckled Renny, grabbing them and shoving them in his mouth.

Hippy John shook his head sadly, "Let's try in that sunny patch by the pool, maybe the frost hasn't got there yet."

Even though nobody apart from PJ thought there were any here, we still kept our eyes on the ground, scouring the white powdery grass. If there had been anything there, we probably wouldn't have seen them anyway. Who could spot white caps in white frost? Nobody that's fucking who. Not even the two John's who were seasoned shroomers. Searching the sunny area proved fruitless too, so we abandoned the hunt, sat down, turned our attention to the calm waters of the pool. Even Renny seemed to be captivated by its shimmering colours. Throwing him a peace sign would have been funny, but I didn't want to put him off.

PJ rocked forward on his heels, "Just think, Lord Byron himself swam here in the 19th century. I've heard all the family stories; he was at Trinity College in 1805. It was the year before Napoleon destroyed Rome. Three years after Britain declared war on France. The very same year Byron got a blowie off the lovely Lady Caroline Lamb..."

Renny and me shared a glance, "He's gone again," said Renny, hauling himself up.

"Yep, come on Renny, let's go," I concurred, already walking.

No sooner had we got a safe distance from the ramblings of the maniac, we sat down.

Renny took out the remaining piece of Thai stick, "Tah dah."

"That'll do nicely," I returned.

Renny dextrously rolled while I looked on. The bloke was a pro, there was no doubt about it, as within minutes he had a decent looking cone ready.

"Shall we offer them some?" I said casting my eyes across the diamond blue pool.

PJ stood up, wriggled out of his jumper and tossed it to one side.

"Er, Renny. Look."

"What? Oh What!! What are you doing PJ?" He called over, lighting up.

Not hearing or not wanting to, he stripped bollock naked and began to wade out into the shallow water of the glistening pool.

"Jesus Christ," I declared.

Renny and me dashed back around the pool to Hippy John.

"Fucking hell man why didn't you stop him?" Renny challenged.

He shook his head in disbelief, "He just got in. I thought he was messing around."

When PJ got to the middle, he dived in headfirst, vanishing in the icy water.

"You're a good swimmer, Skinner..."

"I'm not going any fucking where, I'll catch pneumonia."

"Come on, he's going to drown."

A few moments later he resurfaced, spat out a mouthful of water geyser like, and began waving at someone on the other side of the pool.

"Good morning! It's a family tradition, you know," echoed back across the pool to us.

"Oi don't think you should be in therrrr.'"

"No, it's OK, I'll be fine. Byron's blood runs through my veins."

From behind a gnarled oak tree, the ruddy faced farmer appeared, followed by a gang of other ruddy faced farmers. They belted towards the bridge. In the face of the advancing horde, the penny finally dropped, and PJ turned tail and ran for all he was worth. He splashed back towards us looking like a twisted cross between *The Night of the Living Dead* and *Baywatch*.

"Jesus Christ," I declared, "I'll never unsee that."

"Come on PJ, come on my son, come on come onnn," Renny cheered him, like he was Red Rum at Aintree."

Something hit me on the shoulder, knocking me backwards.

"Those cunts are chucking stuff," I cried out.

Next to me Hippy John ducked, "They are as well."

"Yeah, I know," shouted Renny launching a huge flint towards the angry mob who were now thundering onto the bridge.

PJ surged passed us, skinny legs pumping hard, then he stopped, picked up a rock of his own and chucked it, "Take that you inbred bastards."

Hippy John went to grab one too, but I grabbed his arm. "There's no time, we've got to go."

There was no stopping PJ though, he was absolutely fuming, so much so that Renny had to drag him away.

"I'm mad, bad and dangerous to know," he bellowed.

Under a hail of fire, the four of us sped away from the pool.

Renny got back to the van first, followed by me, then Hippy John and finally PJ. Expecting to see the horde breaking through the tree line at the edge of the meadow at any moment, we piled in, but there was nothing. No movement. Not a sound. It was completely still.

Hippy John started the engine, "I don't like it. It's too quiet," he mumbled, gasping for air.

"OK, Michael Caine, this isn't Zulu, come on let's get out of here," Renny gasped back.

"Where are they?" I asked, chest heaving.

Hippy John spun the camper van around and there they were, tramping towards us from the top of the meadow. Behind them, the gate was shut.

"Now what are we going to do?" Whined Hippy John, clearly shitting himself, "We need to find another way out," he answered his own question.

Hippy John bumped us around the edge of the meadow, looking for a gap, but there was no other way out. Then, he came up to an opening to the pool, slowed and then stopped altogether.

"If I can get onto that bank over there," he told us pointing, "that'll get us back onto the road, I don't know, I'm ... I don't ..."

"Do it then," commanded Renny, "but you'd better do it quick, because those five thumbed fucks are corralling us in like they do with rabbits at harvest time."

PJ leapt up, "No! I w-w-won't have it," he spluttered, his shrivelled maggot-like cock about a foot away from my face.

"Euurgh, Jesus Christ, put something on for fucks sake," I said reeling away.

"It's only a penis Skinner, we all have one, you know!!" He chortled, then he ripped a curtain from the van's side window, and wrapped it around himself,

"Sorry Renny, but r-r-ruining my ancestor's pool i-i-i-isn't an option," he continued.

"Oh, fuck this, I've had enough. Bloody hippies," said Renny, "Get in the fucking back now," he ordered Hippy John.

Hippy John nodded sheepishly and complied, while I hopped over into the front. Renny settled himself into the driver's seat.

"Just drive at them, they'll get out of the way, you watch," I told him.

Renny put his foot down, turned away from the sacred pool and aimed the camper van at the approaching mob, "Yeah exactly. Not even they're that stupid."

"Fucking hell, there's even more of them now," I said in wonder, "there must be twenty of the bastards now."

Renny accelerated, steering at the first two but they weren't going anywhere. They stood their ground, shouting obscenities, then at the last second, they hurled themselves out of the way, raking cricket bats down the side of the van. Then something big hit the windscreen, and a spider's web-like crack appeared, causing Renny to hammer the brakes on.

B.BAAAANNNNGGG, went the engine.

Every one of them hit the deck.

I cracked up laughing, "Do it again, do it again. They think we've got a shotgun."

BAAAANNNGG

B.BBAAAANNNG

Renny shouted, "Hold on tight!" as we raced towards the five-bar gate.

Hippy John's head popped up, "What are you doing?"

"Escaping, what do you think I'm doing Ghandi? I'll show the cunts some civilisation."

"What about the gate? Stop, stop, please stop," shrieked Hippy John.

"Fuck the gate," cackled Renny changing down.

"Nooooooooooooooo."

Bracing myself, I grabbed hold of the door handle, and we ploughed into the gate. There was a massive crack as the wood gave, then we were on the track.

"My camper van," whinged Hippy John.

"Oh, shut up, it's fucked anyway; it's only being held together by cannabis resin."

PJ, still shivering, patted him on the back,

"C-c-calm yourself J-J-John at l-l-least Byron's Pool is s-s-safe."

"My poor, poor, camper van," lamented Hippy John.

Renny kept his mind on the road, ignoring the wailing and thrashed the engine to the centre of Grantchester. Then he turned right and headed for the A 10. On the long approach road to the village, we saw a ruddy faced farmer dressed in Hunters and a Barbour coat walking towards us. Renny and me exchanged a glance. It had to be done.

B.BAAAAAANG went the engine and the farmer nearly jumped out of his skin.

"Come on let's get out of here," said a grinning Renny.

Hippy John asked, "Skinner, turn up the heating, will you? PJ is going to get hypothermia."

"Yeah, sure mate," I smiled reached forward and flicked the switch,

"Well PJ, you've got your highlight for today."

PJ nodded thoughtfully, "We all do Skinner. We are mad, bad and dangerous to know."

THE PROVERBIAL.

Natty was crying again. She'd cried a lot when Den had come back - and little wonder. The atmosphere in the flat had been strained to say the least, but as the days went by, things began to settle down and get back to normal. I couldn't have held a grudge even if I'd wanted to; I was too knackered after work for a long-drawn-out war of attrition. Caitlin didn't seem to have much choice either; a blazing row would bring Den into it. Whether Den would have believed my side of the story I didn't know, but he'd only been back a couple of weeks, so it was unlikely Caitlin would want to risk him leaving again. Natty was also a big factor in us drawing a line under our problems. She was a little ray of sunshine, brightening our world. Natty was always larking about and finding fun in everything. Her interaction with both of us meant it was impossible for us not to communicate, impossible not to repair those bridges. Why she was crying I didn't know, but it was better than listening to Den and Caitlin's early morning shag fest. I rolled over onto my side, checked the time. The clock on my bedside table told me it was seven fucking thirty in the morning. Way too early to be awake on a Saturday, especially this Saturday. I had a big day ahead of me. Back in the village, some of my old mates needed sorting out with a bit of herb. Normally that wouldn't take very long, it was usually knock and drop, but I was dry. I needed to resupply from Lenny's, and you never knew how that would go. It would probably mean the whole morning would be gone. Deliveries completed, I was hoping to give Stink a runabout on the estate, then chill out with Pete and a couple of smokes in readiness for a gig at the 100 Club later on. Natty's sobs petered out, so I rolled back over and tried to get back to the dream I was having. It was one of those scattershot dreams that seem to make sense at the time but when you wake up it's just isolated images. The images were of my VFR and the village. I soon drifted off. Not long after I fell into my slumber, I sniffed a couple of times. There was a smell of rotten meat in the air. Wherever or whatever it was coming from, it was close. Too bloody close. Slowly opening my eyes in the half light of the room, I sat up. Stink was doing his impression of an upside-down footstool at the bottom of my bed.

"You stinky bastard. Stink, get off the bloody bed."

The footstool stretched extravagantly, then he looked up contentedly. He wasn't going anywhere, so I flipped the duvet from under him like a conjuror and he tumbled onto the floor.

"Cheeky git, how many more times?"

Stink gave me a reproachful look, then stalked off to guard the door.

"Yeah, that's right, do something useful," I told him as I got out of bed and started dressing.

Caitlin was doing the washing up in the kitchen when I came downstairs. She was wearing that short black nighty of hers again. I sighed as my eyes traced the back of her long dark athletic legs. In the early days when she had first moved in, I used to think she was just relaxing being at home, but as time went on, I realised that she was doing it on purpose. It certainly kept me and Pete compliant, and I reckon it kept Den on his toes as well.

"Morning Caitlin, you alright?"

"Oh, hi Skinner, sorry about Natty this morning," she said turning around, revealing the Den bump. The little alien seemed to be doing well. Very well.

Quickly averting my eyes from the spawn of Den I said, "Don't worry about it, is she OK?"

"Yeah, she's OK, it's just kids, it's the way they are sometimes."

Nodding, I grabbed the kettle.

Caitlin turned back to the sink, "I know it's short notice, but can you do me a favour? Can you look after Natty this morning? I need to go out."

"Nah sorry, I'm supposed to be sorting my mates out, I'm busy."

"Please Skinner, I'm really stuck. I've got a check-up for the baby. I can't trust Pete he's always stoned, and Den, well you know what Den's like; he's bloody useless at the best of times."

"Yeah, OK then," I said meekly, "I'll get my guitar down."

Oh well, I thought, the lads in the village will have to wait. It would probably work out better anyway. If Robbo was out of herb, then it would be unlikely that Pongo - his contact - would be able to make it over until the afternoon.

"Thanks Skinner, you're a darling."

Natty came skipping into the kitchen with Stink yapping at her heels.

"Morning uncle Skinner," she laughed.

Caitlin cracked up, "Uncle Skinner!!" She repeated, spinning over the empty washing up bowl in the sink.

"You don't have to call me Uncle Skinner - just Skinner is fine Natty."

"OK, affirmative," she said giving me a salute.

Caitlin picked her daughter up giving her a big cuddle and said, "Natty I'm sorry, but I've got to go out this morning darling, mummy needs to see the doctor about the baby. Will you be OK with Uncle Skinner?"

"Not you as well! How about we play guitar? We haven't played in ages, have we?"

She buried her head into her mum's shoulder. "Don't care, I don't want to."

Caitlin and me exchanged a glance.

"OK, er, how about we watch TV then?"

"No, we can't go in there can we Natty, daddy's sleeping, isn't he?"

"My daddy is sleeping in there," she echoed.

I thought yeah, you're back on the smack alright Den, you fucking degenerate bastard.

Caitlin looked at me imploringly.

"I know," I said, "How about we take Stink for a walk? How does that sound?"

Natty looked down at Stink thinking about it, then finally after an encouraging nod from her mum she said, "Affirmative."

"Well, that's settled then, I better get a shift on," said, Caitlin.

Soon as I'd had a bit of breakfast, we slid Stink's new Sid Vicious studded collar over his neck, attached his new lead and tugged open the door.

"See you later, Caitlin," I called out, while Natty said, "Bye mummy," nervously.

There was no reply, so I shut the door on the warmth, and we walked out into another blustery day autumnal day.

Natty stopped suddenly and burst into tears, "I don't want to go, I want my mum," she howled, looking back at the flat.

Bending down, I looked into her eyes, "Come on it's going to be OK, look! Stinky wants to go walkies, look."

Natty looked through her fingers at the over-excited terrier.

"Come on we'll go to the swings, yeah? Yeah?" I encouraged.

Natty nodded, "Affirmative."

'Affirmative' I thought, that's the third time she's said that. Where have I heard that before?

Then it came to me. It was that little girl Newt in the *Aliens* film. Surely, they couldn't have let her watch that. Could they?

"Natty do you know who Newt is?"

"Yes, she's a little girl, she was hurt by the aliens," she said sadly.

Not expecting to hear that, I was shocked. It was hard to believe anyone would let a nine-year old watch a film like that. In places it was so brutal, it had scared the shit out of a lot of adults. No wonder she'd been crying that morning.

"They were bad aliens, not like PT."

"Who? Oh, you mean ET? Like... ET phone home?" I mimicked in his voice.

"Yes PT, he was a nice alien."

"He went home to his daddy and mummy, didn't he?"

Probably not the best thing to come out with, as her daddy was slabbed out, smacked off his face in the front room, but when I glanced down at her she was too busy watching Stink. He was leading the way through the dancing leaves, nose down sifting through the grass, hoovering up the scents. On the path in the run up to dog shit alley the leaves were piling up in mounds. Hoping that none of the Farm's dogs had dropped their cargo early I kicked one of them. Orange, red and yellow leaves exploded into the air, joining the dance. Natty shrieked with excitement, kicked a mound herself, sending more flying into the air like geysers. Stink turned and came belting back through them as they swirled tumultuously to the ground. This carried on for another ten minutes or so, then we moved on towards dog shit alley.

Natty looked up at me, her cheeks apple red after our excursions, "Do you like my mummy?" she asked.

"Y, y, yeah, of course Natty," I admitted, taken aback by the question, "Why?"

Natty giggled, then ran, expertly weaving her way through with Stink in pursuit. Once I had hesitantly made my way through, I stopped and watched in horror as she bounded towards the burnt-out roundabout. Ed Ridley and his mates were sitting on the burnt-out shell.

"Natty!!" I called out into the blustering wind, my voice urgent, "Natty!"

She came to a skidding halt, "What's the matter?" She called back, clearly puzzled by my tone, "What is it?"

"Natty? Come back here now!"

Ed and his mates were already up on their feet and walking towards her. Natty shrugged her shoulders, turned and skipped towards them. Stink didn't seem to care much either, he was heading for the long grass at the back of block six. I ran as fast as I could but was too late. All I could do was get myself between her and the advancing gang.

"Hi Natalie, are you alright?" Smiled Ed, friendly enough.

"Hiya Eddieee," she cooed back, then ran off giggling.

To be honest, I was so stunned I hardly noticed Ed and his mates dossing me out as they stomped past.

"Skinner? Skinner? Can you push me?" Implored Natty leaning back excitedly on the swing.

Exhaling, I strolled over, still stunned by what I had just witnessed.

Stink ran about like a lunatic while me and Natty had a go on the swings, the rocking horse, and the slide, then as the lunatic tired, we headed back. On the way, I tried to process what had happened. Ed walking by like that made no sense. None at all. I was vulnerable, a sitting duck. One thing I knew about Ed, his older brother Ridsey and their steroid bloated mate Jason Brown was, if you were defenceless, showed any fear or worse, tried to turn the other cheek, they'd always steam in. They couldn't help themselves. Fear to them was like a red rag to a bull. Natty and Ed seemed to know each other, how, I didn't know? It must have been from school. Maybe Ed had a little brother I didn't know about. Still, it didn't explain why they didn't do anything, it wasn't as if Stink was about either; he was way off. He always saw danger, why hadn't he seen it then? No, I couldn't work it out. Nothing made sense. Stink was the first back to the flat as usual. Caitlin opened the door on his first bark, and he belted over to his water bowl to quench his thirst. The three of us stood back laughing at the racket the little fella was making lapping it up. Soon enough the bowl was empty, so I filled it up while Caitlin got Natty ready to go to the shops. Raising her eyebrows at the closed sitting room door, she told me she needed to get some fresh air. Understanding, I pulled a sour face and nodded.

"Thanks for this morning," she said, doing up the toggles on Natty's red jacket.

"No problem, it was fun."

Caitlin gave me a big smile, "What do you say Natty?"

"Thank you, Skinner," beamed Natty. Then, they were gone with the wind.

Dirty fucking Den, you low-life rat bag, I thought, as I turned from the sitting room door and began to climb the stairs, going up to my bedroom. There was no way I wanted to bump into him. Not after spending the morning looking after his stepdaughter. Most of the time I wasn't sure whether to hate or pity the bloke, but at that moment in time, hate was winning the bout. A few moments in my room alone would probably be for the best. The best for everyone. Just as I got comfortable on my bed, Stink poked his head around the door, nosed it open and settled in his usual place on guard duty. I snorted at the silly thing. Him sitting there like that reminded me of the day he first latched onto me. The day of the death trip. I thought a bit of music would be good, and what better way to remember that day than the Twinkle Brothers *Dub Massacre*. Hauling myself up off my bed, I made my way over to my stack system and began sifting through the albums. Thankfully, my album collection had grown again since I'd sold the lot after leaving home, so it took me a while to go through them all. I couldn't find it though; I must've gone through them four or five times. To start with, I thought I was going mad, but as I went to go through them again, it occurred to me that just after Den and Caitlin moved in, Pete's albums had started disappearing. Pete hadn't pressed the point, he was a mellow bloke and didn't think Den would do something like that, but the more I thought about it, I was sure it was down to him. To be one hundred percent sure, I slowly went back through them one last time, stacking them up on the floor next to me. It wasn't there. I even checked under the stack system, around the back of it and finally under my bed. There was nowhere else it could be. I sighed, ran my hand back through my hair and noticed my guitar had been moved too. After playing, I always rested the flying V against the wall, keys out. It was the other way round; the keys were touching the wall. In seconds, I was down the stairs. I booted open the door of the sitting room and marched in. Pete was lolling back in his chair engrossed in the TV as usual, while Den lounged on the settee with his feet up on the coffee table.

"Oh, alright Skinner," he said, shifting uncomfortably, "What's up with you?"

Pete pried his eyes away from the screen.

"You seen my Twinkle Brothers album, Den?" I snarled.

"What do you mean?" He retorted aggressively, taking his feet off the table and sitting up.

"You know what I'm talking about, the album you fucking nicked," I told him, moving in.

"Honestly, I don't know what you're talking about Skinner," he whined, rocking back again.

"I know you've been nicking albums. You had Pete's as well. Didn't you?"

"Honestly Skinner, on my kid's eyes, I didn't take it."

"Nah course you didn't. You remember Pete?" I said, turning. "When your albums went missing?"

Pete frowned, looked away. "Don't bring me into this Skinner, it's nothing to do with me."

"Cheers mate," I sneered.

Den got up, "Oh, I've had enough of this, I'm going for a piss," he said, "Honestly I haven't seen your album, you can search my room if you like."

"Yeah? yeah, I fucking well will then," I told him shadowing him.

Pete grabbed my arm as I strode past, "Come on just leave it, he hasn't got it. You remember that Smith's album that went missing, it turned up at one of my mates' houses," he hissed.

"Did it?"

"Yeah, just hold on a minute."

Now I was getting confused. Nah, I thought. Den must have it, there's nowhere else it could've gone. All of my mates were into punk or metal. Nobody I knew liked dub reggae. There was no way it was around any of my friends' houses.

A few minutes later, Den strolled back in with a big grin plastered on his face,

"I'm not joking Skinner, I haven't had your album, I'm not like that, if you want to check my room, help yourself."

"Yeah, I might just do that. Fuck it, I'll check now."

Back up the stairs I pounded, but instead of going into Den's room, I went back into mine to check one more time. What Pete told me must've got through. Even before I'd got to the stack system, I could see the album's red cover sticking out about an inch from the rest of them. You fucker, I thought and ran back downstairs, taking them two at a time.

"Do you think I'm stupid? You just went up there and put the album back," I seethed, going for him.

Den protested, "No, no, I didn't I promise. I went for a piss, on my kids..." backing off.

"Eyes?" I finished for him.

"OK, on my mum's grave it wasn't me, maybe Caitlin had it, or Natty?"

Enough was enough. Prodding his pigeon chest with my finger I got right in his face.

"You are a lying cunt. It was you, just admit it, I'm going nowhere until you do."

Den dropped his head, "OK, OK, OK, I took it, I heard you playing it. It was good, I just borrowed it OK? I was going to put it back."

"Yeah, sure you were," I raged shoving him onto the settee, "I fucking knew it. Don't go in my room again Den, and don't touch my fucking guitar again," I shouted, making for the door.

"No, I didn't touch your guitar, I didn't."

"I mean it Den, stay the fuck out of my room," I shouted, slamming the door behind me.

Den and Pete were talking in hushed tones in the living room when I came downstairs to go out. Despite the fact that I knew what he would be saying, I wanted to listen, to find out what the snake was actually saying, but I forced myself towards the front door.

"I know Den, I know mate, he can be like that sometimes. He was well out of order," echoed into the hallway.

Exactly what I didn't want to hear, exactly what I expected to hear. Everyone I knew had been through this with Den. He would fuck somebody over, then turn it around to make himself look like the victim. He'd done it to me on several occasions and more fool me, I'd stuck up for him believing he would never do it to me. He did though, a few quid here a few quid there, a favour here a favour there, it soon mounted up. Even though deep-down Den was a good bloke, any empathy I had for him was long gone. I had warned Pete when Den had moved in, but he hadn't listened to me. To tell the truth I hadn't listened to the warnings either, so why would he listen to mine? He would just have to learn the hard way like the rest of us.

Pete appeared out of the living room, "Skinner, hold on, hold on, that was well heavy man."

"Sorry Pete, I'm due up Lenny's place, I need to get some herb," I said, knowing full well that he wouldn't want to slow me down.

Pete nodded his head, and I made my way to the door. As I stepped out, Stink went bombing past me into the yard.

I sighed, "Come on boy in, you've had your walk."

He just looked at me.

"Den's worried Skinner, he needs help," Pete's voice came from the dark of the flat.

"Come on then Stink," I said, ignoring him, closing the door on the inevitable outpouring of misguided sympathy that was coming my way, "If Renny's there, you can bark at him," I chuckled, looking down at the little maniac weaving through the spindle like washing lines.

Black Death's cover had nearly blown off in the wind. Great gusts were throwing it up in the air like the sail on a yacht. I reattached the bungee straps as tightly as I could, and then the two of us continued on to Lenny's place. Robbo hadn't been seen down on the Farm for a while. Rumour had it that business had been so good, he'd bought himself a nice four-bedroom detached house in a quaint little village outside of Royston on the Herts/Cambs border. Stink hesitated as we came up to Lenny's, then trotted up and gave the door a sniff over. It looked brand new. Expensive too. It even had a brass knocker. Standing back, I checked to see if I'd got the right place. No doubt about it, it was Lenny's alright, so I leant on the freshly painted blue door with my shoulder. It wouldn't budge; it was locked. In all the years I'd been going around Lenny's it had never been locked before. I dropped the solid metal weight onto the lion's head, thinking Robbo must be spending a bit of cash doing the place up too. Tracy opened up and I stepped into the kitchen with Stink following closely at my heel,

"You alright Tracy? You look nice, are you off out somewhere?" I simpered, clocking her heavy makeup.

She gave me a tight smile, "No," she spat, "I wish, I was."

Tracy could be off sometimes; the scowl on her face told me she definitely didn't want to talk today.

"Is Renny about?" I asked, on my toes.

"Yeah, there're all in there," she nodded towards the living room.

I smiled, "Thanks Tracy," I said stepping inside, then stopped.

The kitchen had been cleaned up. It was still worn out, but the sink was empty, the sides were clear, and someone was in the process of painting the Artex ceiling.

"Bloody hell," I muttered taking it in.

"Through there," she said, pointing impatiently.

"Right. Cheers," I carried on into the living room.

On the settee sat the biggest skinhead I have ever seen. Even sitting down, you could tell he must've been about six foot four. He wasn't lanky either, he was well filled out, like he'd been pumping iron, and hitting the punch bag regularly at the gym. Behind him hung a black and white portrait of Adolf Hitler. Ridsey and Aiden sat on the cramped settee with him, while Renny, Shads and Brandon sat opposite on three new chairs.

The big skinhead leaned back to glare at me, "You must be Skinner! I've been looking forward to meeting you... I heard you're a dab hand with a rolling pin?"

Ridsey said, "Yeah, and that ain't over."

The big skinhead put his hand up, "Let's set it right. Your mate, Jason Brown, Jace, came out of the dark and jumped Skinner. He had every right to defend himself."

What the fuck is going on? I thought.

"This is Kipper," Renny told me, seeing the confusion etched on my face.

"What brings you around here?"

"Is Robbo about?" I said, finally, finding my voice.

Kipper chuckled, "Robbo's got a prior engagement."

A couple of the lads laughed.

Aiden grinned at Kipper, "You won't be seeing him about Skinner, not for a long time."

"Are you here to buy drugs?" Kipper asked, looking me up and down.

"Yeah, a bit of weed."

"Bit of weed, is it?"

"Drugs aren't for us Aryans; that's for the other lot, the macaroons."

Aiden and Ridsey nodded in tandem. Well, that's bullshit I thought, Ridsey is a speed freak and when Aiden isn't slabbed out on the brown, he's doing coke.

Kipper folded his heavily tattooed arms pushing the muscles out, clearly enjoying himself.

"How's Natalie?"

"Natalie?" I replied.

"Yeah, my daughter, Natalie - you live with her and her bitch of a mum."

I paused, stunned.

"Are you fucking deaf or something?" He challenged.

"No, I mean, yeah, she's fine mate."

"Mate, is it?"

"She's fine."

"Natalie tells me you're teaching her how to play guitar?"

I breathed a sigh of relief, thinking that the game of cat and mouse was over, "Yeah, she's coming on well, m... she's really good."

"Good," he answered taking a deep breath himself, "Are you taking drugs in front of her?"

The cat was back playing with the mouse again.

"No, no, course not. Look, sorry, I need to get moving, we've got a gig haven't we Renny?" I said, trying to get out.

Renny shook his head, "Nah, it's been postponed until next Saturday. Listen Kipper, I'll walk him out, put him in the picture," he added after a short pause.

"Yeah, you do that Renny."

He nodded, got up and made his way over.

Stink stood up too.

'Grrrrrrr.'

"Shut it Stink," I told him.

Kipper cracked a smile. "Why have you nicked Hillsey's dog Skinner?"

"He's not Hillsey's, he's Basher's. Hillsey was just looking after him while Basher was inside, I'm looking after him until he gets parole," I blurted out.

"Yeah, so I see, but we need a guard dog to protect my gaff from all the druggy scum around here. You can leave it here."

"Oh no, come on, he's happy where he is."

"He's a dangerous dog," he told me, glancing at Ridsey.

"Yeah, he went for my little brother, didn't he Skinner?" said Ridsey, the snide.

"No can't have that. I don't want a dangerous dog near Natalie... What kind of a dad do you think I am?"

"He's fine with her, he only attacks people he doesn't like."

Kipper pointed a chubby finger in my direction, "Tell you what I'll do for you Skinner. And I'm only doing this because Natalie likes you. You leave the mutt here and if it doesn't work out you can have it back."

"No, no. No way," I said.

Kipper stood up, seething, "The fuck did you say?"

Stink snarled.

Renny seized my arm, "Come on Skinner, do what he says and just leave the fucking dog."

"OK, OK, OK," I said, stepping back.

Stink stuck by my heel. Gazing down at him I said, "Stink, you stay here boy."

I went to leave, and he followed me, "Come on mate you'll be alright," I whispered.

Ridsey laughed, "Oh dear, are you crying Skinner? Boo hoo..."

"Fuck off Ridsey, you cunt," I exploded, going for him.

In a second, Kipper was on me. He grabbed the lapels on my leather jacket and smashed me against the wall. Then he lifted me off the ground. "Whose fucking mutt, is it? Whose fucking mutt?" He shouted crushing me.

Struggling to breathe, I wheezed, "He's yours... Kipper."

"Correct. He fucking is. Now fuck off, before I damage you," he shouted, dropping me like a bag of shit.

Ridsey grabbed Stink by the scruff of his neck while Renny led me out.

Stink whimpered. Then he was gone. Not long after we were out in the orange lights of the Ridgeway, I let it all out. I couldn't help it. My head was in melt down.

"What the fucking hell is going on?" I cried.

Renny rounded on me, "Skinner, for fucks sake pull yourself together, don't let people see you like this, it's embarrassing mate."

"I don't fucking care."

"What you want Ridsey to see you like this?"

"That cunt is dead."

"Yeah, well, that's more like it."

Every part of my body ached; my chest heaved, trying to pull enough air into my lungs. It wasn't enough, nowhere near enough.

"That's it, take a minute, suck it up, calm the fuck down, you didn't want that dog to start with anyway."

"What?"

"You need to choose your battles more carefully; that's not a battle you're going to win. Forget the dog and stay away from Lenny's."

Nodding, I took a deep breath, "I can't believe he's out. I heard something but... Didn't he get life for Little Duggs?"

"No, it wasn't life, he got ten years but there was a re-trial and one of the witnesses changed their statement. He did his original sentence, two for GBH."

Still badly shaken, I asked, "So where's Robbo?"

"A few days after Kipper got out of the Scrubs, he came back here, smashed the fuck out of him, put him in hospital. Then moved into Lenny's with his kids."

"And Tracy let him?" I cried.

"Did you not notice how much makeup she was wearing?"

I nodded, "That bastard... hold on. What the fuck were you doing there?"

"I was knocking out those Halfords tool kits we nicked."

"You're not going to deal with that bastard, are you?" I exclaimed.

"Listen. Don't start on me. I've got no choice, I can't look after my Nan on my own, she needs around the clock care, I'm getting someone in to help. It's fucking expensive."

"You're going to work with the Aryan brothers?"

"I've. Got. No. Choice."

"Get a job then," I raged.

Renny scoffed, "What with my record? I've got no chance."

"Fucking hell, I can't believe you're being serious; you know he'll do you too mate."

"Well, maybe. But until that time comes, it's business as usual."

Not for the first time that day, enough was enough,

"Fuck this, I'm off."

"Skinner? Oi?" Skinner? I'll let you know about that gig later, yeah?" He called out as I reached my yard.

"Yeah. Whatever," I mumbled, and walked back into the darkness of the flat, alone.

CHAOS U.K.

Hertford North station was busy at this time of the evening, so it was easy for Pete and me to walk through the barrier and out onto the platform without being accosted by a ticket inspector. Brandon, Shads, Renny, and his new girlfriend Alice were standing halfway down the platform, leaning against a wall puffing away on roll-ups. Renny raised his hand, nudging the others when he saw me and Pete dodging around the other passengers towards them.

"You alright Skinner? Glad you could make it," he welcomed me sincerely.

"Well, I'm not going to miss the U.K. Subs, am I? I haven't seen them since 1982."

Everyone said hello to Pete, after I had introduced him, and then we stood lounging, waiting for the next train to come along.

"You two got tickets then?" Renny fanned a handful of freshly bin dipped tickets.

"No, oh I'm so sorry! We didn't have time to get them, the train was pulling out," I pleaded, using the statutory reply for ticket inspectors.

Pete took one of the tickets in his hand and turned it over, "Bloody hell, this is a ticket for today, where did you get them?" He marvelled.

Everyone cracked up laughing at his innocence.

"You haven't lived, have you?" Laughed Shads.

Renny always had a pocket full of train tickets. If he didn't use them going to gigs, he would knock them out to his mates. Or, if he was feeling charitable, he would give them away for free. I slipped mine into my wallet and Pete followed suit.

"Cheers Renny. Is this a freebie?" I grinned hopefully.

He smiled, "Yeah sort of, I'll take it out of the money that we made on those Halfords tool kits," he said cautiously, knowing what was coming next.

"Oh yeah, how's it going working for the Fourth Reich?"

Shads frowned, looking me up and down, "You know that twat, Pongo? Where he goes the Pong goes? He only came round Lenny's offering Kipper a load of Thai sticks, didn't he?"

Renny nodded, "Yeah well, he won't be doing that again in a hurry."

"No, he fucking won't," smirked Shads, smiling at the memory.

I shook my head sadly, "For fucks sake. He was alright, he was."

"Was, is about right," continued Shads, "Fucking should have seen the state of him, he was a proper two and eight."

Pongo wasn't the worst dealer I'd ever dealt with, nowhere near it. He was friendly, intelligent, a good laugh, liked punk rock and most importantly he knew his weed too. If he had something good, he would always pass it on, but now it looked like we wouldn't be seeing him down on the Farm any time soon. Renny and me exchanged a glance. There was no doubt about it, we were thinking exactly the same thing. We'll have to find someone else, someone as good, or the people we sell to will be giving us grief. The train thundered into the station.

"Renny? How much did you get for those toolboxes?" I shouted over the ear-splitting din.

He gave me the same tight smile he always did when he was divvying up, then he fished a couple of crinkled twenties out of his pocket and handed them over. I put them in my back pocket, knowing that would be the last time I went out thieving with him.

"Watch this," grinned Brandon, wrenching open the door on the slowing train.

He grabbed the inside window ledge and rode the door along the platform until the hydraulic brakes hissed the train to a stop.

Bemused passengers quickly made their way to the other carriages while the rest of us jumped into the carriage behind Brandon. Soon the train got underway, and we sat back and watched Hertford rush past the filth encrusted windows.

"Who's up for a little drinky poos then?" Purred Alice wiggling a Coke bottle from her pink cuffed PVC military jacket pocket.

Everyone nodded and began pulling bottles and cans out of their jackets, everyone except Pete who looked on forlornly. Alice took a long swig then handed it to Pete.

"W-what's in here?" Stuttered Pete.

"It's vodka, I love the smell of vodka first thing in the evening," she replied.

"You love it anytime, sweetness," said Renny pinging up the ring pull on a purple can of Tenants Super, grinning over at her.

"Go on, it's alright - dive in Pete," she insisted.

Pete upended it, downing four or five big gulps before handing it back.

"Fucking hell man," said Brandon holding up his purple can in response.

"Easy Pete. You don't drink, remember?" I ribbed him.

Pete winced at the aftertaste, "It's been a shitty week."

Shrugging, I swallowed a large draft of my Taunton's extra dry cider,

"I'll drink to the back of that."

Pete was right, it had been a shitty week, and we all knew why, even Shads. Not that it would have bothered him. What was our dog to him? Nothing. If it had been his dog, then maybe he would've known what we were going through. Out of all of us, I was probably the lucky one. It had been so busy at work that I had little time to think about our missing friend, but the others had. Caitlin and Natty had spent a lot of time crying, while it looked like Den was using it as an excuse to dig deeper into the brown. Pete had seemed alright;

he was a mellow type of guy even without the weed, but seeing him knocking back the alcohol like that, told me he wasn't. Both of us had put on a brave face and carried on like nothing had happened, but deep down we were both in need of some kind of release. Tonight was the night, time to let loose and have a good time. No matter the consequences. And there were bound to be some where we were heading. Kings Cross was the end of the line, so we piled off, fed Renny's bin tickets into the barriers and jumped on the escalators down to the packed platform. Brandon exchanged a nod with Renny. I thought, I hope they're not thinking of doing what I think they are.

Renny moved in close and whispered, "You're on window duty Skinner."

They were, "For fucks sake," I said to nobody.

Brandon swept through the hordes of people searching for a mark. Even before he had got halfway down the platform, I'd seen her. With her shampoo and set, back-combed hair, and blue business suit adorned with a pearl necklace, she was a proper Thatcher clone. He always picked out the Thatcher types, he hated Thatcher even more than the rest of us, and with good reason too. He had relatives in the old mining towns of Wales who would never work again because of the iron malady. Shads had seen her too, gave us all the nod and we all moved in on the unsuspecting Thatcherite, waiting for the tube to come. A few minutes later, the tube came hurtling out of the tunnel and then amidst the screeching of hydraulic brakes, it came to a halt. It couldn't have stopped in a better place. The door rasped open. The Thatcherite got on through the single door at the end of the carriage. I followed her in with Renny, while the rest got on through the double doors further down. Then they got into position, moving around her, waiting for the tube to pull off. Oh, for fuck's sake, I thought I'm not in the mood for this. I just want a night out, have a few bevvies and a decent laugh. There was no stopping them though, not now, so I forced the grime encrusted window down in readiness. The tube slowly moved off, thumping over the fish plates, then picked up speed. Soon, it had got up to full speed and it began to scream as the metal wheels negotiated the curved track. Through the swaying heads, I could see Alice striking up a conversation with the Thatcherite. The screaming of metal on metal made it impossible for her to hear, so she leant into her. Seconds later, a royal blue designer purse was handed to me. Brandon had dipped her handbag, passed her purse to Renny who stripped it bare, then it was down to me to drop it out the window. I turned, flipped it, and watched it disappear in the darkness between the buffeting carriages. Nobody had seen a thing. They never did. Everyone was too engrossed in their own lives: worrying about their performance at work, the silly amounts of money they owed on their houses, and a million other self-made problems, that they never saw what was going on right under their noses. Even if they did it was unlikely they'd want to get involved. The Thatcherite alighted at Warren Street, while we carried on to Oxford Circus, where we rolled off the tube in fits of laughter.

"How much did we get Renny?" Asked Brandon keenly.

"Hold on, hold on," he grinned.

Renny plucked a couple of fivers and some pound notes from his heavily studded leather jacket pocket, laughing like a mad bastard, "Fucking hell, there must be seventeen quid here. That's the booze sorted for tonight then."

"Brandon, one. Thatcher the milk snatcher, nil," announced Shads, like he was reading out the football results on Grandstand.

"It's always the same score mate," smirked Brandon, spying another Thatcher-like bouffant hairstyle up ahead.

"No, come on let's get to the gig. We're late - we're missing the support band," countered Alice determinedly, marching up the stairs that led to Oxford Street.

"I couldn't give a monkey's, I'm only here for the Subs," returned Brandon, shadowing his next victim.

"How are you getting on man?" I asked Pete.

"I didn't sign up for this," he told me lurching forward trying to swig the last of the vodka from Alice's bottle.

"Nah, nor did I mate. Come on, if they want to fuck around that's up to them."

Brandon and Shads stomped off, closing in on the new mark, while Pete, Renny, Alice and me went the other way down Oxford Street towards the 100 Club. I had never been to the 100 Club, the Vortex or the Roxy, the birth places of punk in the U.K. before. By the time I was old enough to go into London on my own, the Roxy and the Vortex had long since closed. In the early 80s at the age of fifteen I had finally won the battle with my parents and had been to the Lyceum, the Rainbow, the Forum, the Roundhouse, the Electric Ballroom and many others, but not the 100 Club. Tonight was the night to put that right. Renny pulled out his Kodak camera and took a few shots of us posing underneath its iconic sign.

"Come on then let's spend a bit of Thatcher's hard stolen money," grinned Alice, thrusting her hand into Renny's front pocket, "Where is it?" she laughed, rummaging around.

Renny stood there, grinning like the Cheshire cat,

"Keep digging."

"Where is it Renny?" she asked, grinning.

"It's in there somewhere," he cackled, shifting, "Oh whoops, it's in me back pocket," he said after a moment, creasing up.

Alice cracked up too, gave him a playful slap on the cheek, then disappeared into an off-licence around the corner from the venue, while we took in Oxford Street. Nothing changed, day or night; it was like it always was. Cars, taxis and buses all battling for supremacy in the cloud of diesel smoke. Smiling to myself, I watched a despatch rider carving his way through the mayhem. I thought fucking hell, he's working late, but it shouldn't have been a surprise. Quite literally, we worked around the clock. All clocks. My smile grew even bigger when I saw the big glowing sign of HMV. I had been using their security roller over the last few weeks with great success. It had been amazing; my CD collection had trebled. Only problem was, I had mentioned it to the lads at Central Express. Not long after convincing them that I wasn't bullshitting, they all wanted to borrow it; some had even offered me money for it. Nobody was getting it though. That was mine and mine alone. Brandon and Shads showed up as Alice broke the seal on a fresh bottle of vodka, but when she handed it to them, they shook their heads, in favour of the bottles of cider she had bought. They needed to quench their thirst because it had all gone wrong. The mark had been onto them right from the start. When Brandon had dipped her bag, she'd shouted, grabbed her mobile phone and they'd ran like hell. Pete and me exchanged a glance. I shrugged my shoulders while Pete opted for another long gulp of the vodka. He already looked pissed out of his head; I thought we'd better watch him. He'd never been to a punk gig before and the one thing I knew about first timers was, if they got knocked about on the dance floor, they could take offence, get arsey and lash out. For someone like Pete, that wouldn't be a good idea, he would be in for a right pasting. Renny didn't seem to be in good shape either, but he'd be fine. He was a veteran when it came to punk gigs, and if it all went off, it was normally him that was dishing out the pastings.

Alice grabbed my arm, "Come on then, virgin," she said, leading me through the entrance of the hallowed club for the first time.

"Are you de-flowering me, Alice?" I asked, looking into her dark eyes.

"Oooh, chance would be a fine thing, Skinner."

Renny separated us with his elbows, "Skinner's not interested, he's waiting on a call. Who is it now? Mia or Cerys?"

"Could be Ghostbusters," slurred Pete incoherently, "I ain't afraid of no ghost!" He sang.

"Oi, fuck off you lot. Pete, your idea of a date night is a pot noodle and a wank."

Everyone cracked up.

"No, I don't like pot noodles," he slurred, visibly confused, "What?" He cried.

More laughter.

"Skip dinner. Get straight to it, eh?" Brandon patted him on the back, "Good man. You'd better watch him in there, Skinner, he's off his nut."

"Yeah, I know," I agreed, taking Alice's hand, "Now where were we? Oh yeah..."

Brushing Renny aside, Alice walked me down a flight of steps to the ticket office, and after sharing a joke with the person serving, we bought our tickets. Then we carried on down another flight of stairs into the club. My first impression was that it was small, but as I got further into the mass of assembled leathers, tartan bondage trousers, and bright Mohicans, I saw it was bigger than I first thought. Eventually I worked it out. It was like a long hall but instead of the stage being at one end, it was in the middle, which meant the crowd circled the band and could get close. I hadn't seen a stage like that since I'd played with the lads in Virus V1. It was just one step high, but that was the punk ethic. The bands and the crowd were one and the same. Punks onstage played in bands to punks on the floor; we ate the same, shat the same, we were all human beings after all. There was no place for superstar wankers within the punk movement. That's the way it had always been. Alice dragged me over to the bar, with a slightly miffed Renny and the others close behind, where we got the essential for a night at a gig. The first pint glass. No sooner had we got them, we drained the expensive venue drink and put our own pre bought drinks in. Then, grinning like naughty school kids, we moved back over to the right-hand side of the stage near the entrance to wait for the Subs to come on. Not long afterwards, they bounced out onto the stage humbly waving to us. It was brilliant, they were so close you could have shaken hands with them. Charlie was the only one I recognised; the rest were completely unknown to me. I was beginning to wonder if I was going to miss, Paul Slack, Nicky Garret and Pete Davies (the lineup I saw back in the 1980's), when the band launched into *CID*. No chance. The whole place went up like a rocket. Pete, Alice, Shads and Brandon vanished in the mayhem, while I stayed in front of the guitarist and out of the crush, by ramming the bottom of my legs against the low stage. Oh well, I thought, Pete is old enough to look after himself, I'm sure he'll be fine. I swigged my snakebite and passed it over to Renny, who took a swig himself. Then he pulled out his camera. Renny always took a few pictures at gigs, but he seemed keener than ever tonight. Every time Charlie bounded over to our side of the stage; he would take a couple. *CID* ended in massive cheers, then, *Emotional Blackmail* followed, my favourite Subs track. There was nothing else to do. Letting myself be taken by the swell of the crowd, I was dragged into the pit. It was fucking chaos. Chaos U.K. style. I pushed and was pushed, then from behind someone grabbed my collar. Spinning around, there was Brandon, grinning like a maniac. He was holding Pete up. He gave me a playful shove. Pete just gazed straight through me though. He was fucking smashed. He looked like he was about to be sick. Then he was. His head flew up, his mouth lolled open and out it came. It splattered down the back of someone's cloned Discharge leather jacket and onto the floor. Thankfully, the bloke was so engrossed in the music that he didn't notice. Good thing too, it would have been pasting time; he was absolutely massive. Brandon and me moved away from Pete and the puked on jacket, laughing our heads off. But our laughter soon stopped, when Pete toppled over into the mass of kicking legs and stamping feet. Before we'd even laid a hand on him, others had come to his rescue and were helping him back up. Brandon went to drape his arm over his shoulder but saw the diced carrots down the front of his shirt, so he backed off and we made a path to the side of the stage, while the other less aware punks lugged him over.

Pete plopped himself down on the stage and leant into me, "This is fucking brilliant Skinner this is the best gig I've ever been to and you're one of the best mates I've ever had," he told me with breath that would melt paint.

"Yeah, cheers mate," I said raising my glass, "The Subs always do the business."

"I'm sorry I didn't back you up with Den you're right he's an asshole you're a really good mate for bringing me up here."

I smiled at the bloke. He really was off his fucking gourde. "Any time mate, any time," I toasted him, then I heard the first chords of *Endangered Species*.

In seconds I was back in the melee, driving into people, people who understood what it was all about. Being shoved, shoving back, enjoying the release, stamping out the frustration, the anger and the pain. Everything was being chucked onto the filth encrusted floor beneath us, all the angst, the pressure and the bullshit from their insane society, left among the rubbish and the old beer cans. Left for dead. Brandon, Shads and me found each other in the pandemonium during *Limo Life*, another Subs classic, and we raised our hands up and had a proper singalong, then as the last chord faded, I felt thirsty. Fucking thirsty. So I moved to the side of the stage with Renny and Pete. Charlie and the boys lashed into the next track just as I got myself locked onto the stage. Good thing too, as the place went up around me. Breathing heavily, I grabbed my pint off the stage in front of Renny, gave him a nod to thank him for shielding it and downed a huge draft. It tasted good. Refreshing.

Life affirming. I exhaled, then Pete caught my eye. He was still sitting on the stage trying to watch the band, but his body didn't want to be there, his body had had enough. It was not only waving the white flag; it was winding down the flagpole. Slowly, he slumped forward by degrees. It must have been the slowest fall in history. He took two tracks to go from sitting up straight, to lying flat out with his face squashed into the carpet.

I shouted, "Is he alright?"

Renny put his hand on his neck checking his pulse,

"Well, he's still breathing. I think he's asleep."

Renny and me cracked up laughing, shaking our heads in unison. Never before had I seen anybody fall asleep at a punk gig. I didn't think it would be possible, but he looked happy enough curled up underneath the guitarist, so we let him get on with it. A few tracks later, when he woke up, he didn't look too happy though. So with the help of one of the bouncers, we heaved him up onto a chair, back from the stage where he could still see. Pete thanked us with a grunt and was beginning to get back into the music when we left him. Renny still wasn't getting into the pit which really surprised me, especially as Alice had been there from track one. He was quite happy though, watching the band and taking his pictures, that is, until someone with a yellow Mohican got up on stage and started dancing with Charlie. No bouncers came to chuck him off, so that's where he stayed until the track ended.

Renny was fuming, "Get the fuck off the stage," he shouted.

Mohican gave him the two fingers and just stood there, while the band launched into the next track. People started lobbing stuff at him, but he dodged left then right, all the while keeping his fingers in the air. My glass was half full. I wasn't going to waste it on that knobend, so I bent down, scouring the floor for something else I could chuck. Rummaging through the sticky detritus, it wasn't long before I came up trumps. I thought, this will shift him, lobbing an empty purple can at him. It bounced off his shoulder and he gave me the wankers sign, but he stayed put. Finally, at the end of the track, Charlie asked him to get off the stage and he gave the crowd a sarcastic bow and departed. Renny was still furious, he forced his way over to him and smacked him one. Mohican fell backwards, disappearing from my view. Renny pushed his way back, wiping his hands, then, from nowhere two blokes jumped him from the side. One of them punched him in the face and he fell backwards, clattering into some other punks who pushed him upright. The other bloke moved in on him, so I got between them.

"Fucking leave it," I told him.

The one who had punched Renny stepped back, but his mate stood his ground, steadily dossing me out.

I shouted, "I mean it. Fuck off, dickhead."

He was going nowhere, he kept on staring, so I shoved him backwards, then a couple of bouncers appeared and separated us. Now the bouncers were here, he lunged at me, but they were too strong, they grabbed him by the arms and disappeared in the crowd. I checked Renny, he looked dazed, confused even. He scratched at his chin. Then rubbed his hand over his cheek, checking for any damage. For the life of me, I couldn't work out what his problem was, he was always on the other side of a fight: the winning side. Tonight though, he just didn't seem to be with it at all. I hadn't seen him drinking any more than he normally did. I was bewildered. It just didn't add up. Renny ran his hand down the side of his face for a second time, then shrugged his shoulders, picked up his camera and got back to taking pictures of the band. Charlie and the lads played four tracks as their encore with the last one being *Kicks,* and I made sure I was at the front for that. Even though I was worried about my mates, I was determined to get every bit of pleasure out of tonight, because who knew what was going to happen tomorrow. Kipper? Bike crashes? Poison mushrooms? Cancer? Or maybe the superpowers would push the button, and it would be over for everyone. One thing you could be certain of, was everything and anything could happen. Renny led the way out and just as I suspected, he waited for the Mohican and his mates. I don't know where they went, maybe they had been chucked out by the bouncers earlier on, but after twenty minutes or so they still hadn't come out, so we decided to leave. Pete was unsteady on his feet, so me and Brandon put his arms over our shoulders and walked him up the bright lights of Oxford Street, while Renny and the others stumbled on behind us. One foot in front of the other, we struggled along until we got about halfway to Oxford Circus, where I spotted a Porsche 911. I let go of Pete and did something I'd always wanted to do since my first day as a despatch rider. I put my foot on its low bonnet and skipped over it like I was trip trapping over the Ogre's bridge in the Brothers Grimm tale. Everyone cracked up laughing, and soon everybody wanted to have a go at it. It turned into a full-on procession. People were gawping at us as they went past on the bus, but we couldn't give a fuck. We went back and forth over the yuppie German monstrosity until Brandon saw some blue lights coming from the bottom of Regent Street. Game over, it was time to move on. Brandon and me grabbed our charge and edged off towards the tube station. Once we made it to Oxford Circus, we had a decision to make. Who was going to take Pete down the stairs to the top of the escalators and how? My old man used to give me something he called a 'fireman's lift' when I was a little kid. He would bend over, I would fall over his shoulder, then he would stand up. No doubt, it was simple and effective. Whether it would work with two people of a similar size I didn't know, but I thought it would be fun to find out. I leant forward as my old man did, Pete went over my shoulder, but he slipped down my arm and fell into a heap on the pavement. Everyone was in stitches, except Pete. He looked confused. He was totally fucked up. On the second attempt, he managed to keep his balance, so I tentatively stepped down the steep stairwell using the handrail to steady myself. Pete wasn't that heavy, so it wasn't too bad, and it was funny looking at the Londoners, laughing at us as we struggled down. At the bottom, I slid him off and pushed the ballast towards Alice and Renny, hoping they'd help out. To start with, they weren't having it. As far as they were concerned, he was my friend, so he was my responsibility. In the end, I decided to test them out, see if they were the decent people I believed them to be. I sauntered off by myself, telling them if they didn't take him, then he'd be sleeping on Oxford Street that night.

Renny was cracking up laughing. He was all for it, but Alice felt sorry for the shy stoner and linked arms with him, "Aw, come on now, Pete," she cooed maternally.

Breathing a deep sigh of relief, unburdened now, I strode on ahead with Shads and Brandon, while Renny and Alice helped the poor fucked up and wasted Pete.

Brandon turned to Pete and sang at the top of his voice, "Crashed out, out of my head."

I knew that Exploited track, so I joined in, "Crashed out, my brain is wasted."

Soon everyone joined in,

"Crashed out, I'm nearly dead."

Pete dry heaved then gave us the thumbs up.

Coming to the top of the cavernous escalators I asked, "Are you two going to be alright with him?" Then I stopped.

Down by my foot there was a brick-like mobile phone, I bent down, picked it up and put it to my ear, "Hello? Is there anybody there? Hello?" I enquired, grinning at the others.

"Fuck, that's a Nokia Cityman, careful that's worth a few quid," cautioned Renny.

"Cityman? I chortled, "Oh, hello Rupert, yes, yes, buy, buy, buy," I said in a posh voice, stepping onto the moving stairs, ignoring his imploring looks.

"You yuppie bastard," laughed Brandon,

"Fucking toss it."

Pretending to lob it, I smirked at Renny.

Shads cracked up, "Toss it, toss it, toss it," he chanted.

"No, no, no, that could be worth a monkey," shouted Renny.

Slowly putting it back to my ear I said, "Get off the line there's a train coming you Eaton cunt," and wacked it onto the balustrade, cracking it open. Then I held it, watching the others.

Everyone was laughing their heads off, except Renny who just gaped at me, his face saying, 'Don't do it'. I did it. The brick-like phone slid down between the escalators, picking up speed and breaking up, showering people with its electronic innards. Two girls screamed as it smashed into the 'No smoking' sign next to them. Even Renny was creasing up now. Somehow it got stuck, so Brandon legged it down and got it going again. It whipped down the last thirty feet at an alarming rate of knots, did a poor impression of a Winter Olympics Ski jumper at the end of the balustrade, then smashed into a million pieces at the bottom.

"You know what Skinner, that was worth five hundred quid just to see," conceded Renny as he and Alice hauled Pete up to me.

Alice shook her head sadly, "Now we'll never know if Rupert bought those shares."

Brandon said, "Fuck Rupert."

"Yeah, fuck Rhubarb," agreed Pete as he struggled past.

Out on the platform, we sat Pete down making him comfortable while we waited for the next tube to arrive. The board above told us it was going to be two minutes. I'm not sure how it began, but Brandon and Shads started going on about politics. I couldn't be bothered with politics at the best of times; it was a fucking waste of time, especially on a night out. It was a complete buzz killer, and it never ended well, not for anybody. I thought it was totally out of order, so I tried to tune it out, but unfortunately it started getting in. In the past, before the coming of Kipper, Shads had kept his views to himself, but it looked like Hitler was in the charts again, and he was buying the records. Only a couple of minutes late, the tube flew out of the tunnel, blasting hot air into our faces and screeched to a halt next to us. The door slid open, and we heaved our charge in. There were loads on board, so we decided, that with only one stop to go, we would stay by the doors. Still the debate carried on.

"Brilliant night," I said, desperate to change the subject, "What's up with you Renny? I thought you'd knock those blokes out."

Brandon turned away from the stream of politics and moved over to where me and Pete were standing, "No chance, he's been in the Griffin most of the day," he told us clearly relieved.

Renny laughed, "Yeah, I've been on the piss since 12 o'clock, I couldn't punch my way out of a paper bag. Even Pete could take me now," he said looking at him over my shoulder.

Seconds later, the tube pulled away, jerking hard. Renny's eyes bulged. Alice cracked up laughing. I turned to Pete to see what was so funny, but he'd gone. I spun all the way around, and there he was, on the deck between a group of seated passengers, grinning up at them. Everyone fell about laughing. Pete slowly got up with as much dignity as he could muster. Then he gave his audience a tiny wave, grimaced and struggled up the carriage back to us.

"Pete, that was classic mate," I laughed shaking his limp hand, "I'll never forget the look on your face, looking up at those people."

Pete chuckled, "It's all anarchy, isn't it?"

Renny creased up, "If only I had my camera ready. Can you do it again?"

Alice pecked him on the cheek. "Aw, leave him alone, the poor thing" she said, then dropped to her knees in hysterics.

Everyone was laughing except for Shads; fuck knows why, but for some reason he was back on Brandon's case, and he had turned the volume up. Soon, the carriage forgot about the rowdy, yet amusing pissed up punks and tuned into some of the worst crap I've ever heard. Shads was full of hate, his diatribe peppered with the words 'darkies', 'sambos' and 'coons.' Putting my hands over my eyes, I peeped through my fingers. There was a black family sitting just down from us and you could tell by the look on the parents' faces that this wasn't the first time they'd heard those words. Nowhere near it. I was hoping they would get off at Warren Street, but they didn't, the doors remained open, and they just sat listening to the pathetic ramblings.

"Listen Brandon, you don't get it. Our culture is under threat."

"No, it's not, bloody hell Shads it's still here, it's all around us, we just have more cultures, it's made the country better."

Shads pointed an aggressive finger, "Bollocks Brandon, there are too many people in this country," then he pointed down the carriage, "if those lot weren't on here, we'd have seats."

"Oh, fuck off Shads," I said, rounding on him.

"Facts Skinner, there are too many people on this tube," he informed me as the doors began to slide shut again.

"Well, get the fuck off then," I told him, pushing him off.

Shads hit the platform, rolled onto his side, and gaped up as the doors shut. The carriage went silent. The tube pulled away.

Alice put her hand over her mouth, "Oh my, oh my," she whispered and let out a nervy laugh.

Pete patted me on the back, "That was cool, I'll never forget that."

Renny cracked up, then shook his head, "Nice one Skinner," he said grimacing, "but considering Kipper and him are good mates, you might live to regret that."

"Ah, fuck him," I said, "Nazi punks fuck off.

THE BATTLE OF MIDWAY.

Inside the warm cafeteria, people sat in groups; families, the young and the old, exchanging pleasantries, enjoying the adventure of being on a voyage. Not me, though. I had never felt so alone, and my mind was in turmoil. That morning, I had left the hotel in Calais in good spirits, anything seemed possible. Everything seemed possible. There was only one thing I needed to do. Act natural, blend in, don't bring attention to myself, but I had fucked it up. I'd fallen at the first hurdle. I had ridden to the port, bought my return ticket, then gone onto customs, stopped at the barrier and waited at the window as the sign had instructed. A few minutes later a woman appeared and said, 'bonjour'. I replied, 'hello'. Immediately switching to English, she asked me for my passport. Handing it over, I then heaved off my crash helmet. She checked it over, then satisfied she nodded and handed it back. To the side of the checkpoint, a door opened, and a customs officer appeared. He went around the back of the bike, lifted the lid on my top box, had a cursory glance inside, then he dropped it, gave the woman a wave and walked off. That was it. I couldn't believe it; it was so easy. He hadn't even checked my panniers. I'm through I thought, I'm fucking through, what was I worried about? Either they don't give a shit, or they are fucking stupid. Didn't give a shit? Fucking stupid? Whichever one it was, I was through. Relief, excitement, elation, and a million other emotions rose up inside me. I was so happy, I almost laughed, I had the biggest smile on my face. In front of me the barrier that had once stopped me flew up. I went to wave at the woman in the window, then I saw the look on her face. Questioning, suspicious, she was wondering why I was so happy, so elated. My wave stalled and my face dropped, but it was too late, the damage had already been done. I had fallen for their little ruse. If I had been just a normal passenger, there's no way I would've been so relieved, so happy, so excited, to be waved through. Even as I pulled away, it still hadn't quite clicked. It was only when I got on the ferry and had calmed down, that I put it together. Every time I saw that expression on her face it became more damning. France was a long way behind me now, whatever happened, had happened. It was over. Done. It wasn't the problem. The customs in England were the problem now. If the French customs alerted them, then they'll be ready and waiting for me as soon as we docked at Dover. There won't be any cursory glances in Dover, that was for sure. They would tear my bike apart. I was slowly, but surely, sailing into a fucking trap, a self-made fucking trap, at that. On the wind battered deck a young couple ambled in front of me holding hands, carefree, breathing in the bracing sea air. In that moment I hated them, hated their easy manner, their happiness; everything about them repulsed me. I knew I wasn't thinking straight. Nowhere near it. So I got up and made my way to the front of the ferry, where I found a dryish seat, sat down and tried to reign in my careering mind. The white cliffs of Dover were clearly visible now. It wouldn't be long. I had never felt this kind of anxiety in all my life. It was tearing me apart, crippling me. All I wanted to do was get it over with, get it done, no matter what the outcome. If I was going to get caught, then let it happen. Let it happen now. This was fucking torture, and it wasn't being helped by the swell of the sea. As the ferry crested the high waves, the white cliffs looked closer, then as it dipped down the other side, the cliffs fell back and seemed even further away.

"Excuse me," said a woman in her early forties, "Is there anyone sitting here?" She smiled gesturing to an empty chair next to me.

"Yeah, go on then, whatever. Take it. I couldn't give a shit."

Exchanging a look with a bloke I assumed to be her husband, they then moved on despondently, pushing a little kid in a wheelchair, to a row in front. Even though the wheelchair bound kid was severely disabled, I felt jealous of him. Jealous that he had little or no responsibilities. That he didn't have to look after himself. That everything was done for him. Even though his body was warped, broken and out of shape. In that moment, I wanted to be him. No, I didn't want to be him. I hated the little bastard, him and his soppy fucking parents. All of them. Everybody. No, no, no, that wasn't right, I was going fucking mad. My head was in meltdown, I had to stop this, had to stop it now. I shuffled over to the railing and looked down into the churning grey waters below, thinking about ending it all. Do it now. Do it. Finish it. No one would miss me, I was a piece of shit, a piece of shit who had got involved in something I was ill equipped to deal with. Now my fear was manifesting itself in the form of hatred, hatred of decent people who were just living their lives. What a fucking low life. If I leant forwards a bit further, I'd go overboard, be swallowed up by the unforgiving sea and that would be it. No more pain. Do it. Do it now. Finish it. I couldn't go through with it. Life is precious, a gift not to be squandered. I didn't want to die. Who does? Only a fool. There had to be another way. Then it came to me. Why not ditch the coke in the sea? Then there would be no trap. This feeling would be gone. No more pain. Head down, fighting against the wind I made my way back along the deck. I lugged open the heavy door to the cafeteria, felt the warmth, breathed in the smell of freshly cooked bacon and eggs. I thought, I'm on a mission here and there is no stopping me, but when I came to the top of the stairs that led to the car decks, I stopped to think. Going back to the U.K. empty handed would mean trouble, big fucking trouble. The fallout would spread far and wide. People I cared about would get hurt. Selfishly, inevitably, I put my DM on the first step that led down, then picking up momentum, I almost ran to level two. Hesitating for a moment at the steel doors, I tried to remember where Black Death was. If I spent too long searching the car deck, someone would see me and that would be it. Racking my brains, I tried to remember, then it came to me, the VFR750 was on level one. Taking two steps at a time, I sprinted but as I got near the bottom, a bloke in uniform appeared coming up.

He frowned, then gave me that suspicious look, "What are you doing down here?" he challenged me.

"Oh, alright mate?" I returned, completely caught off guard.

"You shouldn't be down here; it's not permitted; there's a sign at the top of the staircase."

"I need to get something out of my bike mate," I told him.

"Nobody's allowed down here until the ferry docks. For security reasons and safety reasons.

Those doors must be kept shut," he said with finality.

Nodding, I turned tail and began walking back up. There it was again, I had behaved differently to a normal passenger, I had done something to stick out. This time it was in front of an official on the ferry. Someone who would have a direct link to the port authorities in England. Someone like the customs officer in France, who had been trained to notice passengers behaving strangely. I felt like a right fucking idiot, because I'd behaved like one. If they didn't know before, they certainly knew now. Back on deck, I made my way towards the bow and as I went, I took in the passengers again. It was like nothing had happened. They were doing what they had been before. For them it was a day out, a nice cross channel trip, something they would remember for years to come. No way, I didn't hate them. How could I? After all they were just living their lives. I didn't hate anybody, apart from myself, for getting into this mess.

WEST ONE (SHINE ON ME).

Central Express' rider's room was packed out which was unusual for midday, let alone on a Friday. All but two of the riders were in: Bile Ball Bob our resident Jehovah's Witness was plotted up in SW1, while the other, Frances, the company's stand-up comedian was up in NW1. Nobody was missing either of them, both of them were a pain in the arse.

"I'll just shift these," chuckled Nev as he swept a pile of *Watchtower* magazines onto the floor, making some room for his tall skinny frame on the bench.

Muttley laughed, "Oi Nev, that would've made some good toilet paper."

"No, it's too shiny mate, it would just spread the shit around," he returned, tracing his hand back through his sun-bleached hair.

Graham's head popped out of the controller's room window, "If it carries on like this, we may as well go home," he stated forlornly.

Jez, Graham's giant son joined him at the window, blocking the view into the radio room.

Chuck eyed him, "Are you sure Jez switched the phones on this morning?"

"Yeah, yeah, it's quiet because nobody's calling us," said Jez defensively.

Everyone cracked up. Yacob scratched his wiry black beard,

"If we go home now, do we still get paid?"

Graham laughed at his audacity, "Yes, I'll get my limousine driver to drop you off."

"I've never seen it so quiet!" Declared Damo mournfully shaking his head.

"I'm so bored. I might have a look at this load of shit," I scoffed, booting the shiny copies of *Watchtower* across the floor.

Damo laughed, "Careful Skinner, you could be tempting fate there?"

"Nah, Jehovah loves us, he never ignores a repentant heart," I quoted Bile Ball Bob.

Muttley sniggered, "Well, that's you fucked then."

"That's us all fucked," laughed Marco, raking back his long black hair.

Chuck nodded, "Sounds like you've been reading it, have you Skinner?"

Denying it, I shook my head.

Muttley cracked up, "I bet he has too, he's probably been wanking over it."

"Nah, I've got your mum in *Readers Wives* for that."

Everyone fell about.

Damo leant forward, "One of my mates in Melbourne? Told me he tried using all those religious books as bog paper, but they didn't work because they were already full of shit."

Everyone laughed, except Yacob, "You should not say that about people's religion," he said solemnly.

Chuck looked at him challengingly, "He just did mate."

Yacob shook his head, "This is not right."

Now and again Yacob and Bile Ball Bob got shirty about what we said about religion, so we'd stop, change the subject, give something else a hammering. Nobody really wanted to upset anyone, because we were all mates, despatch riders, and part of the same team. But as soon as they'd gone, it was a different story. It was business as usual. None of us cared; jokes were jokes, and where religion was concerned, there were no boundaries. Everyone hated it.

Graham flourished a docket, "Does anyone fancy an ICC Banner Street going WC2?"

Before anyone could move, I snatched it out of his hand, "Cheers Graham, that'll do nicely," I said, copying it into my docket book.

Damo snorted, "Bloody Poms, look after themselves, don't they?" He said to Chuck, who nodded back.

Soon as it was done, I waved my book at them like I was wafting a noxious fart in their direction, then giving the convict descendants two fingers, I strolled out looking like the cat that got the extra creamy cream. None of us riders at Central Express wanted to sit about, it was boring, we wanted to get out on the streets and enjoy ourselves. It certainly wasn't about the money; we were all on guarantees. If you did the five days, no matter how much we earned we would always get £300 a week. If we earned over that like we did most weeks, that's what we would take home. I'm not sure about the others but I never paid any tax, or National Insurance. That was for the fucking mugs, the hamster wheelers. With the package from Banner Street safely in my top box, I raced around the usual route. Left on Golden Lane, right on Fann Street then left on Goswell Road. Fucking hell I thought, seeing the amount of traffic backed up on Goswell Road. It was proper gridlock. Further down, towards Aldersgate, there were blue lights flashing, probably because of another smash. I sighed, then carefully weaved the cumbersome VFR through the stationary metalwork, choking on the diesel fumes, but I only got as far as the junction with Long Lane. There was nothing for it; I would have to cut through Smithfield's Meat Market. Not my usual route, it was to be avoided. It was hard to get any speed up, especially around 2 o'clock when the Barrow Boys were pushing their barrows to the buyer's lorries. It was midday though, so the auctions would still be on going. Watching the lights, willing them to turn amber before I choked to death in the mustard gas diesel fumes, I revved the engine. The lights changed. Dipping my shoulder right, leaning over, I navigated the VFR around the sharp turn and hit the straight of Long Lane at speed. Black Death must have been touching 50 miles an hour when a lorry backed out of Grand Avenue. I dodged right to avoid it, but then from the other side, a Barrow Boy appeared with a big pink pig's carcass on his barrow. He shouted, tugged his barrow left and the bloated pig rolled off onto the road. He shouted and screamed; he was going fucking mental. So I stopped to see if he was alright, and watched in horror as the reversing lorry backed over the pig's carcass. Time to go, I thought, grabbing a decent handful of throttle and getting the fuck out of there. Once I had dropped off in WC1, I was hoping to get something going back in the direction of Central Express, so I could carry on chatting with the lads. However, Graham told me to stay put, because he needed someone plotted up in the West End, just in case a booking came in from that area. Steadily the autumnal cold folded in around me. My almost waterproof Rukkas were still wet from riding in this morning, which wasn't helping either. I needed to warm up before the cold really got in. Knowing London like the back of my hand, I knew just the place, so I hopped back on and rode to Guildford Street, parked up and wandered into Stebbing's Laundrette. Spring, Summer, Autumn, Winter, rain or shine, it was always warm and dry in the laundrette. Nodding a hello at a couple of nervous old dears doing their smalls, I grabbed a pew, unfolded the *Motorcycle News* and perused the for-sale pages, scanning to see if my old Honda VT 500 was still in there. Motorcycle City in Hounslow had sold it to me: brand new in red, it was beautiful. Cheap too - I had traded in my GN 400 and had got a good price for it. Like all things new, I looked after it, tried to be careful even out on the circuit, but when I found it scratched and dented lying on its side after a drop, it wasn't new anymore. Over the next year, I put it through its paces, clocking up over 60,000 miles. The bike would be worthless once it hit 90,000, so I decided to unplug the speedo, freezing the mileometer at 62,987 miles. During my two-year spell working as a lab bike out of WC2, it served me well. Then things started going wrong; just little things to start with, which I got repaired down at Clubhammer's. Time went on and the miles mounted up. It got so expensive that some weeks, I was just working to keep the bike going. The final straw came when it started burning oil, a sure sign the piston rings were going. Clubhammer could have done the job. It wasn't the most expensive job in the world either, but it was time to sell, get a new bike; get that road rocket I'd always dreamt of. Keeping the advert brief, as it was pay per word, I wrote, Honda VT500, red, 62,987 miles, some service history, in good condition. *Motorcycle News* ran my advert the very next week. I sat back and waited, then the following weekend, I got a call from somebody in Hoddesdon who was interested. Sunday morning, him and a friend came over to the Farm to give it the once over. He looked happy with it, but when he asked if he could have a go, I had to be careful. If he had a go, he was bound to give it a good thrashing, and thrashing an engine with dodgy piston rings would only mean one thing. Smoke. Luckily for me, when I asked him for his driving license, he said he didn't have one. He hadn't even passed his test, so I offered him a backy. He agreed and we set off along Longwood Road, with me deliberately keeping the revs low. By the time we'd done a circuit of the Farm, the bike was smoking like a fucking chimney, but unbelievably, the bloke was enjoying himself so much that he didn't notice. His mate did though, and when he jumped off to tell him how brilliant it was. I could see his mate, trying to warn him. He was smitten though. He paid the money over, jumped on his new bike and disappeared in a cloud of smoke. A few weeks later, I still hadn't found my dream bike. There was absolutely nothing within 100 miles of the Farm, so I decided to get another VT500 to get me back on the road, get me earning again. Soon, I found one up in West Hampstead, 40,000 miles on the clock, only one owner, full-service history for £375. I phoned the guy straight away and we arranged to meet the next night. My luck was out this time though; it couldn't have been a worse night for looking over a bike. Dark, windy, it was pissing with rain and freezing cold. I didn't want to hang about, so I gave the bike a cursory glance and checked over the relevant documents. Everything seemed to be in order, so I knocked him down to £325, shook his hand and agreed to buy it on the spot. To get the money together, I'd had to use everything I had. One pennies, two pennies, five pennies and ten pennies. Much to his dismay I handed the seller £300 in notes and made up the 25 quid with the shrapnel. Deal done, I hopped on my new bike, but as soon as I pulled away, I knew I'd fucked up. Fucked up badly. It was like riding a crab; to make it go straight, you had to steer the bike hard left. Obviously, someone had chucked it down the road; chucked it down the road with such ferocity that the frame had been bent out of shape. I turned around, which was really easy to do on that bike, went back to the guy's house and told him I wanted my money back. To start with, he protested, whinging, saying that we'd shaken hands, and the deal was done. I told him what he must've known, it was a write-off, and I wasn't going any fucking where until I got my money back. He soon saw sense, gave me my notes. Then slowly and methodically counted out the pennies into my hand. I counted along too; I wanted every penny back. Still, I didn't have a bike, but not long after that total waste of time, I found another VT500 for sale in Hoddesdon: red, 65,000 miles on the clock, full-service history, in great condition, first to see will buy. No matter what the weather was, come sleet or snow, I swore I was going to give it a proper check over. Although I'd got my money back from the last guy, it was doubtful I would be so lucky this time. This time I might get a good kicking; I probably deserved it last time. Renny drove me over in his BMW, we soon found the place. It was off Lord Street, which I knew from my Virus V1 Days. The hall at the top of the road had been our last gig before we split up. The bike was parked up out the front of the house. It was red, gleaming, beautiful. Nice one, I thought I'll have a good look at it before the spiel starts. I walked up the path. Then I read the number plate. I stopped in my tracks. It was only my old bike. No way could I have foreseen that, but I didn't feel any animosity because he was just doing what I had done. In some ways, it would have served me right if I had been lumbered with it. Snorting, I span on my biker boots, turned tail, made my way to the car. On the way back to the Farm, I told Renny what happened, and after I'd persuaded him not to go back and punch the bloke out for wasting our time, we carried on.

"Charlie, seven zero, seven zero," squawked my radio, bringing me back to the laundrette.

"Seven zero," I replied, grabbing up my crash helmet.

"Seven zero, you're not falling asleep in that laundrette again, are you?"

"Negative," I laughed.

"When you've finished sniffing old ladies' knickers, can you go to Channel 4 W1 going W11, wait and return? And there's more, call me, P.O.B."

One of the old dears gaped at me like she was about to have a heart attack.

I cracked up, sniffed loudly into the radio, and hit the button, "Roger, Rog."

Nicely busy now, I did another six or seven drops, taking in Camden, Chalk Farm, Hendon and Hornsey. Soon afterwards though, the work dried up again. Graham plotted me up in W1. From the radio, it sounded like everybody else was being plotted up in W1 too, so I made my way to our usual meeting place in Soho. Berwick Street was the perfect spot to meet up, there was a parking bay for motorcycles, numerous cafés and most importantly, some of the best record shops in London. Sister Ray, Daddy Kool, Blackmarket, Music and Video Exchange and my favourite,

Reckless Records all had outlets on or around the street. Not only that, it was a good place to sit back and watch the world go by. There were many characters living and working around the area, including the prostitutes who used the basements on Berwick Street as their knocking shops. My suspicions had proved correct, there were six bikes parked in the motorcycle bay, while across the road, standing in the porch of the defunct XS strip club, where a group of bikers. Seeing the usual blocked drain, I grabbed a handful of throttle and raced through the puddle, splashing a tidal wave of water in their direction. They all cracked up laughing, throwing me two fingers and the wanker's sign. Nobody gave a shit about being wet anymore, despite us wearing waterproofs, for the most part, we were soaked through all day long. It was part of the job. Once I had raced the mini circuit of Peter Street, Hopkins Street, Ingestre Place, and Broadwick Street, I parked up, hoisted Black Death onto her centre stand and strutted over to say hello to the lads. Marco, Yakob, Muttley, Bile Ball Bob, and Damo, were deep in conference, while Noel greeted me by waving a gauntlet like glove,

"You alright Skinner? What's the matter with your bike? Did you get it restricted? It looks slower than ever," he laughed looking around at the others.

"Yeah, I've donated one of its cylinders to your Suzi," I parried, joining the group.

Damo was in the middle of one of his black cab stories. He was always falling foul of them, but we'd all had trouble with cabbies at one point or another. Like getting soaked or freezing your arse off in the winter months, it was just another part of the job. One by one, the anecdotes flooded out as the rain poured down and the radio remained silent.

"Oi look, there's Geraldine," smiled Muttley seeing one of Berwick Street's regular working girls going into the café across the road.

Geraldine was alright, if she wasn't busy, she would come over and talk to us, exchange stories and cigarettes. You had to be careful if you were on your own with her though. Sometimes, she would ask you if you wanted business. No thank you would be my answer, but I didn't know about the others. You never knew. Nobody admitted anything, but the odd exchanged glance between her and the riders, told me, some of them had been around the back of the XS club with her. Muttley was my number one suspect.

"Ohhh, she's wearing those red boots, Noel," I grinned suggestively at the Rasta, "Just in time for an afternoon session."

Noel fingered his glasses down onto the end of his nose and looked over the top, "If everyone chips in, I will."

Marco snorted, "In this weather you will freeze your cajones off my friend," he told him, grabbing his cajones for effect.

"If she had a basement, well yeah, I'd go for it," stated Muttley, further arousing my suspicions.

Noel pushed his glasses back up, "I don't care how cold it is man. Those red boots."

Noel was always messing around, but nobody knew if he was being serious or not, so I decided to up the ante,

"I'll tell you what, if we all put a couple of quid in, that'll probably be enough?"

Muttley shook his head, "No, it's 15 quid."

Case closed, I thought.

Noel cracked up, "You pay and I'll play,"

"No that's not fair. Why should he be the one?" replied, Muttley indignantly.

"OK let's draw straws for it," I said, joking.

Bile Ball Bob, the Jehovah's witness, had been quiet so far, but it couldn't last, "No, no, no, come on. I'm not going to be part of this."

"What about you Yakob? You in mate?" Taunted Damo, his face full of amusement.

Yakob cupped his beard, "I am Muslim."

Damo smirked, "Oh well, you're out then mate, no worries."

"I didn't say that," returned Yakob, pursing his lips.

Everybody patted him on the back, except for Bile Ball Bob, "Don't let them corrupt you

Yacob. God is watching," he preached.

Yacob smiled, "Today may Allah be merciful," he said sending us into fits of laughter.

Bile Ball Bob headed to his bike, "One day you'll all be sorry," he spat over his shoulder.

"Drongo," spat back Damo.

Muttley threw open his newspaper bag and began rummaging around for something we could use for the straws. He couldn't find anything, so he upturned his Central Express bag onto the pavement to carry on the search.

"How's this?" he asked, pulling a straw he used as a dipstick from the pile of rusty tools and smeared dockets.

"Spot on mate," chimed Damo.

Noel said, "Wicked man," nodding along with the Aussie.

Muttley turned away from us and chopped the straw into pieces, with an oily pair of scissors. Then the game began in earnest. One by one, the straws were drawn to the sounds of laughter and 'ohhhhs'. Mine was quite long so I had nothing to worry about. With one straw to go, our aficionado Muttleys', Yacob was the clear winner. Excitedly, we waited as Muttley built up the tension. Slowly, he opened his hand. It was the shortest by far. Everybody cracked up, laughing at the audacity of the bloke. It was so obviously a fix, but it was done now, and although Noel would probably have gone through with it, with the rest of us around, nobody else would have. Muttley danced around us laughing like the mad bastard he was, chucking glances over at his prize. His prize had finished her lunch and was standing in a doorway just along from the cafe, smiling and greeting blokes as they walked past. Muttley sniggered like his namesake Dick Dastardly, and put his hand out, waiting for us to divvy up, then as the pound notes fell, his face did too. Back across the road, a bloke had stopped and was chatting to Geraldine. Watching with bated breath, we awaited the outcome. Deal or no deal. That was the question.

"Oh no, no, come on," howled Muttley, as Geraldine took the bloke's hand.

Everybody put their money away; the game was void. As far as we were concerned, if it wasn't happening now, it wasn't going to happen at all. Muttley moped about for a little while, then as a new idea came to him, he began to grin. He told us to follow him.

"Where are we going mate?" Asked Damo.

Muttley casually removed a board off a broken downstairs window of the XS club and jumped in, beckoning us to follow. Noel was next, then the rest of us. Inside the old clip joint, it was damp and dusty, and with the light restricted to a few rays coming around the other boarded up windows, it was hard to see anything. Muttley obviously knew the way though. He carried on in the gloom, with his hands out in front of him, like a blind man. Then at the bottom of a staircase he grinned and pointed upwards. Damo opened his palms. He ignored him and made his way up the rickety flight of stairs, with us following. Below us the stairs creaked, protesting under our collective weight, while above, a dim light from a door guided our way.

Damo sneezed, pulling a hanky out, "Fucking hell, Muttley, you sure about this, mate?"

"Shhhh," hissed, Muttley.

"What the fuck are we doing?" I asked.

"This is bullshit, man," complained Noel.

"Come on, it's not far now, here we go," said Muttley's shadow from the top.

Once we'd made it up the stairs, we shuffled across a small landing, hoping the floorboards weren't as rotten as the stairs, then into what I could only presume was the club's office. There was a musty leather chair behind the desk, and in the corner, there was an old style safe with its door hanging open, long since emptied. On the floor in the opposite corner, there was a sleeping bag and three or four carrier bags, full of clothing.

Muttley was already at the window chuckling to himself, "Come and have a look at this," he called over his shoulder.

Edging around him, I had a look. Down in the alley below, a bloke was standing with his back to us with his trousers at half-mast, while Geraldine kneeled in front of him, working away.

I couldn't help myself. I shouted, "Oi," and ducked down.

Everyone creased up laughing, everyone apart from Muttley, who put his finger to his lips shushing me. He wanted to see more. A few seconds later, I popped my head up again. Geraldine was still working away, faster now, but the bloke was looking around furtively. He'd heard something. From behind me, one of the bags full of clothes came flying past my ear. Ducking down again, I turned and saw Yacob pissing himself, laughing. This time when I peeped the bloke was squinting up at the window, doing up his flies. He saw me. Then he pushed Geraldine aside and scarpered. I thought it was high time we did the same thing. The other lads were way ahead of me, they were already careering down the stairs so much so, that the floorboards in the office were bouncing under my feet. Taking the stairs two at a time, I was near the bottom when I heard a massive crash and ran headlong into Damo,

"Aaaaaaaaaaaaaahhh," he shouted, "What the fuck? My leg."

It took me a while to realise what had happened. One of the steps had given way. Damo was stuck, he was up to his calves in splintered wood, but he soon got over his original panic and he was cracking up laughing. I doubt he'd have been so happy if he hadn't been wearing his thick leather motorcycle boots.

"Why is it always me?" He whined.

"Because your forefathers were criminals," laughed Muttley.

Everyone erupted into laughter, we couldn't help it, then just to add to the hilarity, Graham called him for a pickup in WC2.

He responded with a curt, "Roger," and turned to Marco, "Fuck my luck, eh? A little help please mate."

Marco and Yacob grasped an arm each, manoeuvred themselves into position and heaved with everything they had, but the Aussie was stuck tight. A few more tugs yielded nothing, so we pulled him out of his boots, then as soon as he was free, we wrenched his boots out. Back out on the street, still laughing about our little adventure, we saw Geraldine marching towards us. Damo suppressed a laugh, sneezed, leapt on his bike and quickly beat a path towards WC2, while the rest of us waited on the streetwalker's wrath.

"Oi, you knob ends, it's fucking lucky that sleaze ball paid me first, or I'd get my pimp to beat you lot up," she told us, smiling.

I smiled back, "Don't worry Geraldine love, Muttley here will pay you double next time, won't you mate?"

"Well, he better," she said as her parting shot, then clacked across the street to take her place back in the doorway.

For once Muttley was speechless, but the rest of us weren't, we filled up his silence with plenty of mirthful laughter. He was finding it hard to take, his ego was getting a proper pounding.

"So, Skinner? You still got that HMV roller?" He said, trying to change the subject.

That did the job.

"Yeah, I've still got it," patting my Rukkas pocket, "Why, do you want to give it a go?"

Muttley nodded, "Yeah, I need to update my vinyl."

Surprisingly, after all their bravado, the other three weren't interested. Marco said that he was meeting some mates down the Bird's Nest in Deptford, while Yacob and Noel told us that as it was quiet, they were going to take a slow ride towards home. Not that it bothered me, it was probably better with two because the five of us wandering into HMV with our newspaper bags, would've brought us a lot of attention. Muttley and me strolled up Berwick Street and onto the busy afternoon Oxford Street. Oxford Street was always the same on and off the pavement. People jockeying for position, overtaking, undertaking, swerving, dodging in the dense fumes, trying to get where they wanted, with no concern for anybody, except for themselves. HMV was packed out; it was another perfect day. Strolling over to the seriously overpriced American import CD section, I got to work rolling the security tabs then dropping them into my newspaper bag. One of the first things I learnt about thieving from the big stores was, once you checked where everything is, i.e. the cameras and the security guards, you shouldn't look around all the time. It would just draw attention to yourself. With a decent haul of around twenty to twenty-five CDs safely stashed in my bag, it was time to take the leap of faith. Did the roller work? Many times before, I had walked through the security barriers undetected, but I always felt nervous as I approached them. No problems, I passed straight through and out onto the bustling street. Muttley was waiting in a shop doorway a little further down. Greeting him with a cheery wave of my newspaper bag, which rattled with the haul of CDs, I handed him the roller. Now it was his turn. To get a better view, I made my way across Oxford Street, and set myself up in a doorway opposite and watched him go in. From start to finish, it shouldn't take more than ten minutes. Any longer was asking for trouble. The longer you stayed the more chance you had of getting pinched. The time ticked away.

My radio sparked into life, "Charlie, seven zero, seven zero?" It squelched.

Bringing it up to my mouth, I replied with the standard comeback, "Seven zero."

"Seven zero, ICC Banner Street going Crawley."

Oh no for fuck's sake I thought, he's sending me South, I've done fuck all today and now it's 4 o'clock, he's sending me to fucking Crawley.

Graham called, "Charlie seven zero, ICC going Crawley," with more authority.

Crawley was completely in the opposite direction to where I lived. If you split London in half as a mirror, Crawley would be the exact opposite mirror image to where the Farm was.

"Charlie seven zero? Charlie seven zero?"

Over the years working as a despatch rider, I'd heard lots of jobs like this being given out. In some cases, riders had told their controllers to go fuck themselves and signed up to another company the next day. Not me though. Despite his past, I liked Graham, he was a decent bloke.

"Yeah, Roger, Rog," I replied.

"I'm sorry seven zero, I've got no one else. Everyone has sloped off."

"Roger, Roger," I signed off.

Suddenly, from across the road, the alarm started ringing. Muttley came high tailing it out of the entrance with his newspaper bag swinging insanely in front of him. Not far behind came two big burley security guards. He sprinted, dodging through the crowds like a professional rugby player, but when he turned to see how close the security guards were, he rammed into an old man, knocking him to the pavement. His partner screamed, looking on as Muttley changed course, finding his progress easier at the side of the stationary traffic. Colliding with the old boy had slowed him down some; the security guards were right behind him now, breathing down his neck. He reached into his newspaper bag and started chucking CDs and anything else he could find at them. No security guard was getting paid enough to be pelted with CDs, so they fell back. It looked like he was going to get away. He would've too, but as he turned to stick his fingers up at his failed pursuers, a taxi door opened. He went into it pell-mell; handfuls of CDs flew in the air. The poor sod was a goner. I melted into the crowd, ambled back to my bike, thinking about the Crawley drop. Grey clouds covered the close London sky. It began to drizzle. It was going to be a long, hard challenging ride but as ever, I was up for it. Before I went anywhere though, I needed to sell the CDs in Reckless Records.

CLUNCH PIT.

Sele Farm only had one pub, the Golden Griffin. It had been my local since I had moved onto the Farm, but with Kipper's Kaos Krew in residence, I decided to find somewhere else. Choosing the Black Horse was easy. It was a proper biker's pub, had been since 1960s, and even though the faces had changed, it remained exactly the same. It served strong ales, viscose scrumpy cider, and its jukebox was loaded up with loud guitar music. It was 10 o'clock at night when I pulled up outside the bright lights of the pub in West Street. The Crawley job had turned out to be a fucking nightmare. To start with all was well, the parcel was waiting for me in reception at ICC and I quickly bagged it and got on the road. Even the rush-hour traffic going south wasn't too bad. I coasted through lines of stationary cars with their bored occupants with ease. Croydon disappeared in my rearview mirror as did Purley, but as I came through Coulsdon, the heavens opened. It was only spitting to start with, then it picked up to a steady downpour. Under the streetlights of London, I could just about see through my rain splattered visor, but after I crossed over the M25, got onto the M23, there were no lights and visibility deteriorated. I thought, can this get any worse? Then it hammered down, answering my question. In all my years despatching I had never seen anything like it. The rain came down in sheets. It was relentless, pinging off my visor like shingle. Not only that, but the spray being thrown up by the cars was non-stop. Ice cold water flew at me from all angles. Keeping my line was difficult to say the least, my vision was so distorted. It was like looking through a murky fish tank. Still, I kept the speed up in the 60s, it was pushing it but slowing down to under 50 would bring me another problem. Cars shooting past me, covering me in spray, was bad enough, but if I went under 50, the endless pounding convoy of lorries would catch up. That was a proper no, no; if I came in contact with one of them, there could only be one outcome. Death. I came to the crest of a hill, below, through the torrent, I could just about make out the red snakelike taillights of the traffic, taking a sweeping left turn. A couple of roadwork signs revealed themselves out of the spray to the left, then there were no road markings. Blindly drifting right, I lost my bearings, then BANG, I was thrown backwards, and the bike was in the air. Time stood still. Then the bike came down hard, pitching me forward onto the tank, and the handlebars began to shake violently. Panic rushed through me. The bike was out of control. I was in a death wobble. There was nothing I could do but hang on and hope it righted itself, then finally as the bike decelerated it did. If I had any thoughts of a Friday night on the piss, they were long gone. The only thing on my mind now was staying alive. For my own safety, I moved into the slow lane, then there could be no doubt where the bike was because I could see the edge of the road. Not long afterwards, inevitably, an 18-wheeler began it's slow overtake. Only a few feet away, its grinding wheels cut deep into the river like road, creating waves, covering me from head to foot. It was like riding in a car wash. I couldn't see a fucking thing. Blind and helpless, I just kept the bike straight and held on for dear life, hoping that it would soon pass. Twenty to thirty lorries must have passed me before the orange lights of Crawley came into view. In all its history, I very much doubted anyone would've been so happy to see the satellite town. I was. Fuck was I. It shone out like a beacon of hope. Turning off the waterway, I soon found a garage, had a shifty look at the local map and found the drop, 15 High Street, Crawley. My heart sang, it wasn't far off. Dumping the map before the cashier could start, I hurried out, jumped on Black Death and got moving. No sooner had I pulled up outside the address, I could tell it wasn't the right place. The package was for a company, while the address I was sitting outside was a residential property. Finding a phone box, I dialled Central Express' number, hoping Graham would still be in the office. He was normally there quite late. Rumour had it he was shagging Shirley, the nice-looking receptionist from the TNT office below. Even though I was freezing, wet, and probably a bit jealous, I really hoped he was. The phone rang a dozen times, and I was thinking of giving up, then finally he answered. He sounded pissed off and not just a little bit out of breath. So I thought I'd probably been right, but I wasn't in the mood to take the piss. Keeping it business, I told him it was the wrong address, and he instructed me to wait while he called ICC. A few minutes later, he came back and said it was High Street Horley, not High Street Crawley. Back to the garage I went, then ignoring the whining cashier, who was ready for me this time, I checked their map out again. Horley was a good five miles north of Crawley, which meant because of the cock up, I would do an extra ten miles of miserable motorway riding. Oh well, I thought, at least it's on the way home, and jumped back on the steadfast VFR and got underway. By the time I got onto the motorway, the rain had eased off and I made good progress. I dropped off in Horley with no further issues and got on the M23 heading north. The further north I went, the clearer it got. The road was still awash, but now with full visibility I opened Black Death up, keen to get some miles on the clock. Soon I came up to the first roadwork signs; there was only one thing on my mind, I wanted to know what I had hit. Slowing down a little, I pushed up my rain splattered visor. Motorway Maintenance had been working on the central reservation. There was a raised area about a foot high with kerbstones around it. I had hit one of the kerbstones full in the face but luckily for me, it was one of the lowered ones. If I had hit one of the square flat ones I would have been thrown off. What would have happened after that, I didn't want to think about. In the bright lights of the pub, I breathed easily, took a backwards glance at Black Death thinking we've made it, then I leant on the door and entered the warmth of the Black Horse. Immediately, I began to feel better. Like a human being again. It was packed out with familiar, friendly faces. I sidled over to the fireplace to warm my hands, acknowledging Renny and Alice at the bar. Renny gestured with his hand, did I want a pint? Nodding back, stretching, like fucking, did I? I rubbed my hands together and felt the flames deep in my bones.

"You alright Alice? Cheers Renny," I said, walking up and grabbing a nice fresh pint of snakebite off the bar.

"Fucking hell man, you look like a drowned rat."

"It's a long story," I told him, dragging off my wet Rukka's.

A wolf whistle rang out from across the bar.

"Steady now ladies," I said looking around the bar for the culprits.

Nick, Viv and her girlfriend Astrid, my old friends from the dig, were grinning over. Thrusting my hips forwards, I gave them a smile and the two fingered salute for good measure, then carried on stripping off. I was soon down to my jeans and T-shirt. I had even taken my more than ripe socks off, much to the displeasure of everyone standing near me. Pretty soon all my gear was hanging up near the fire drying out, while I stood at the bar necking snakebite, telling Alice and Renny about my day. Not long afterwards, the bell for last orders rang out. My head dropped, like I'd walked into cheese wire. I couldn't believe it; it was so unfair. My precious weekend had only just begun an hour ago and already my Friday night was over.

"Nooo, I've only been here a couple of minutes," I whinged at Renny and Alice, "I need a proper drink," I told them. "Do you fancy coming back to mine and having a few drinks?" I asked, not without a little hint of desperation.

"No thanks," Alice said, shaking her head, throwing her red flowing locks from side to side.

"Oh right," I said downcast.

Renny chuckled, "She's winding you up, there's a woods party at the clunch pit tonight," he laughed nudging his girlfriend who cracked up.

"Really?"

They both nodded back.

"Yesss," I said punching the air.

The clunch pit was in a large wood that ran out of the back of the small hamlet of Hertingfordbury. It was quiet. It was out the way, and it wasn't far away from the Farm. It was perfect for a woods party. Perfect, to get the weekend started.

"If you're interested," she continued, placing her hand on Renny's thigh.

"Not if you two are going," I smirked and picked up another pint.

Renny put his hand on Alice's, "Tell you what, since you've had such a shit night, we'll go and get a few supplies. We'll meet you there later yeah?"

"He's trying to say thanks, after you saved his drunk arse at the 100 Club."

"Well, yeah cheers mate," I said, a bit embarrassed. I raised my glass up, toasting him,

"You've helped me out in the past."

The two of us went quiet, then Alice burst into laughter, "One day, you blokes will learn how to open up."

Renny and me exchanged a glance and shook our heads, like that was ever going to happen.

Not in our lifetimes, anyway.

"You two," she laughed again.

Kicking out time at the Black Horse was normally a slow, arduous, and sometimes dangerous task for Bill the landlord, but tonight everyone left without a fuss. It looked like word had got around. Thankfully, by then, my gear was pretty much dried out. Grinning at Bill I took my time putting on my thick jumper, leather jacket and warm boots. Then I put my waterproofs under my arm, gave him a sarcastic wave and strolled out to my faithful machine. People were chatting, laughing, jumping into their cars, and hopping onto their bikes. There was only one place to be tonight. All roads led to the clunch pit. Black Death roared into life under me, I kicked down into first, gave it some revs, gently released the clutch and pulled away. From the clear skies above, the moon shone down its ghostly white light while all around the streetlights glistened. I revelled in it. Motorcycling was good again. In the short time it took me to ride to the dense woods that surrounded the clunch pit, I realised one thing. I would always have a motorbike. Motorcycling was in my blood. Cars were parked at jaunty angles, like they'd been left in a hurry, in the car park at the entrance to the dark woods. I was about to park up between Renny's BMW and Hippy John's Commer camper van, when I remembered the last time there was a party here someone had their motorbike nicked. Thinking, fuck that for a game of spanners, I carefully weaved around the chaotically parked cars and made my way to the path that led into the woods. Keeping the speed low between ten and fifteen miles an hour I coaxed the road racer along the muddy path. Even at those low speeds, the mud was so cut up by the amount of people who had come this way, the VFR was making heavy work of it. In the distance through the oaks, hawthorns and horse chestnut trees, I saw the orange glow of the fire. Twisting the throttle in excitement, I found the back wheel skidding, so I moved off the sludgy path onto firmer ground. Dodging between the fallen branches, bushes and small saplings, I came to the edge of the bowl like pit. Surrounded by thick vegetation, I could see the top of a blazing fire, its twisting flames turned the white unmined chalk a light shade of orange. To the left of the towering inferno, a boombox blasted music, while black silhouettes gyrated, dancing around it. Never before had I seen so many people at the pit. It was a welcome sight. I thought, what are you waiting for? Let's go, the weekend starts here. I slipped the bike into gear and eased it down the edge of the bowl onto the pit floor. There were seven or eight other bikes parked up at the bottom of the slope, so I stuck mine next to them and heaved my aching body off the saddle.

Even before I had a chance to take off my crash helmet, Caitlin came running up to me shouting, "Skinner!" Excitedly, and she wrapped me in her arms.

Feeling my resistance, she stepped backwards. "Skinner, this is cool I can't believe I'm out; my sister is looking after Natty! I'm freeeee," she sang, inadvertently touching her baby bump.

I smiled back at her, attaching my crash helmet to my seat lock and said, "Sounds good, where's the booze at? Renny reckoned he was bringing some?"

"He's over there, come on let's get you drunk," she giggled, towing me over by the hand.

Renny and Alice were chatting away avidly but when they saw me coming, they immediately clammed up, looking guilty.

"Skinner," Alice greeted me.

I snorted, "You alright? What's up with you two? What are you talking about?"

"Nothing, nothing," dismissed Renny telling me it was something, something.

Caitlin grabbed my hand and insisted, "Come onnn, let's dance, I want to dance, come on."

"What is it Renny?" I carried on, ignoring her pleas.

Alice nudged Renny, gave him a nod of encouragement, "Oh, it's nothing..." he said, "but, well, I saw that mutt of yours, up at Lenny's. He didn't look in a good way."

"What? What's up with him?" I asked, dropping Caitlin's hand.
Alice nudged him again.
Renny sighed, "OK, he started acting up. Kipper put him in the shed at the back of Lenny's."
"But he's alright, isn't he?"
"Yeah, yeah, yeah, he's a tough little git."
"Yeah, he is," I agreed, "but what do you mean he was acting up?"
Renny gave Alice a look, "Don't worry about it, I shouldn't have said anything. Tracy will look after him, she loves dogs."
Caitlin sought out my hand again, "Of course she will, she'll see him alright," she assured me, pulling my hand, "Listen, if I can survive living with Kipper, I'm sure he can," she said finally and tugged me over to the dancers.
Encouraging me with a big smile etched on her face, she started bopping about, getting right into it. I started moving too. Then I stopped myself. Thinking about the last time when we got close. How she lied about losing the baby. How she mugged me off big time. Then most damning of all: the cold, calculating, conniving look on her face, when Den told me she was going to have his brat. I muttered, 'No fucking way,' more to myself than anyone, and marched away. If she heard me, I couldn't have cared less. She'd humiliated me. Bulldozed me. Strolling through the other partygoers, I suddenly felt out of place, like I was bringing the whole thing down. After the pub I probably should've gone home and relaxed. Given it a miss tonight. I'd been in the saddle for twelve hours. Fuck it, it was time to go, so instead of going back to sit with Renny and Alice, I changed direction and headed for Black Death.
Nick, Viv and Astrid were checking out the bikes when I strolled up.

Astrid saw me approach and waved, "Which one's your bike? Is it this black one?"

Giving her a perfunctory nod, I went to unlock my crash helmet.

"Can I have a go on it?" She asked hopefully.

"Yeah, sometime, yeah," I returned distractedly, fiddling with the lock.

No matter where I went, or what I did, everyone wanted a go on Black Death, everyone asked, but they had no chance. In fact, it got on my nerves. Why would I risk that?

"OK, give me the key then," she said with not just a little bit of surprise in her voice.

I snorted, "Now I know you're fucking joking. You couldn't even ride my bike on the road, let alone here," I said, sure in the knowledge that she hadn't done her test.

"I'll have you know. I'm a very good rider... Watch this," she said, throwing her leg over a raked out old Yamaha RD 350.

Now I had thrown down the gauntlet, she had something to prove, and fuck did she. She gave me a patient smile, twisted the throttle, got the revs up, then she let the clutch out and went shooting up the bank, throwing dirt all over us. Wheelieing at the top she spun around on a sixpence, then she skidded to a halt and waved down to us, laughing like a fucking maniac. Nick then jumped on his bike, a scrambler, and joined her at the top where they beckoned me to join them. There was no way I was going to take Black Death off road any more than I had to. The VFR wasn't built for chalk pits, it was a thoroughbred, built for the open road. With a shake of the head, I sat down and watched them as they tore around the bowl. It looked like a right fucking laugh. Soon, I was tempted to join in. Even the people dancing had stopped to watch. Nick would go to one end of the chalk bottomed bowl, while Astrid waited at the other. Both would rev their engines furiously, waiting for the signal. Viv would wave her jumper in the air, like the girl in *Rebel Without a Cause,* and they would race at each other. Only at the very last second, would they change direction, sending the partygoers into rapturous applause. I beckoned Astrid over, and after one more pass, she sped up to me and slid to a halt.

"Give us a go then," I asked, thinking she'd probably tell me to piss off, like I did when she asked, but to my surprise, she grinned and hopped off.

"Cheers Astrid."

"Remember, keep the revs up at all times," she instructed.

Nodding my head confidently, I chucked my leg over the lightweight two-stroke and grabbed some throttle. I knew the RD 350 well enough. I'd never owned one, but it was familiar to me. It was one of the three bike week. The rev counter bounced up to 3 o'clock, I dropped the clutch and went hammering up to the top of the hill. No fucking way was I doing passes with Nick, so I rode around the bowl a few times, then, satisfied, I pulled up in front of a grinning Astrid.

"OK, now you do a pass Skinner," she said, "All you do is go right; he will go left. It's the same every time."

Easy enough I thought, you'd have to be a complete moron to fuck that little trick up. Powering up the bank as Astrid had done, I spun it around at the top and waited for the signal. Everybody was watching intently. The jumper dropped. I snatched a handful of throttle, let go of the clutch and hurtled down the bank and out onto the floor of the pit towards the fast-approaching Nick, who was pulling a wheelie. At the last moment I veered left. He went right, and we zipped past each other. No problem. Simple as ABC. I cracked up laughing. There was no doubt about it, it was fucking brilliant. I wanted to go again, but when I turned to Astrid, she waved me over.

Her face was a picture of horror, when I skidded up in front of her.

"You were supposed to go right!! What the fuck happened? Get off."

"What really? Jesus fucking Christ, it's lucky I didn't," I sniggered, hopping off.

First the lowered kerbstone, now this. Someone doesn't want me to die today, I thought.

Astrid shook her head, "Lucky, lucky, Skinner."

I smiled, "I was born that way," I told her, "Can we…"

"Shush," she said suddenly, putting her finger to her lips.

"What's up?"

She pointed into the woods, "Listen."

Torches shone down on us from above, lighting us up. Before I could work out what was happening, Astrid came shooting past me on her bike, drawing the torch beams. Then I worked it out. It was a raid. Police were streaming down the banks left right and centre, their torches tossing light in all directions. I threw myself into some bushes and lay down flat, as a group of them in Hi-Vis reflective jackets came belting past. There were shouts from near the fire and the music cut off. Through the dense undergrowth I could see torches tracing the progress of Astrid as she climbed the bank at the other side of the pit. Then she was gone. There were more footsteps pounding in my direction. I froze. Then there was a shout and whoever they were, stopped. Peeping through the greenery, I saw four partygoers with their backs to me, coppers with torches stood in front of them, highlighting them. One of the partygoers whispered, "chuck it," and four or five little bags hit the bushes around me. First of all, I ducked, wondering what was going on. It took me a while to figure out what happened but when I did, I put my hands out, blindly searching around for their discarded stashes. Nettles stung my fingers; the little bastards, so I gave up the futile search and tried to see what had happened to Alice and Renny. Notebooks and pens out, some of the Police were taking down people's details at the fire, while others were trying to put it out. Then I noticed another group of Police with torches making a sweep of the bushes at the bottom of the bowl. If I stayed put, they'd probably find me, but if I broke cover, they'd definitely see me and the chase would be on. And there were a lot of the bastards out there. In the end I decided to make a move, there was nothing else for it, I'd have a better chance that way. Doubling over, I cautiously made my way out of the bushes towards Black Death. In the shadows behind the gleaming row of bikes, something moved. I froze, steadily watching. A few moments passed then a figure appeared moving towards me. Whether they'd seen me or not, I didn't know but I wasn't taking any chances. Reaching down I grabbed a decent handful of soil. Whoever it was, they were going to get a fucking face full.

"Skinner? Is that you?"

Caitlin wandered out of the shadows.

Breathing a sigh of relief, I put my hand up, "Caitlin? Are you OK?"

She ran up to me put out her arms like she was going to embrace me.

Backing away I said, "Leave it out, we need to get the fuck out of here. Now."

She laughed uproariously,

"Oooh, are we in trouble?"

Even in the low moonlight I could see she was well buzzed up. I didn't know whether she knew the danger we were in, or she just didn't care. It was probably a bit of both.

I whispered, "Keep it down, Caitlin, take my hand."

Now sniggering like this was a game, she put a milky hand out. I reached forward, grabbed it, then led her through a group of saplings towards the bikes. Suddenly, we were spotlighted by a torch. Both of us froze like statues. Seconds passed, then the beam swung away, and we carried on to Black death. Unlocking my crash helmet from the seat lock, I handed it over to Caitlin, threw my leg over the bike and kicked the back pegs out for her. Caitlin awkwardly rammed on the crash helmet, got on and wiggled in behind me. The group of Police who were searching the undergrowth trained their torches onto the bushes where I'd been. They would be upon it soon. It was now or never. I pulled the clutch in, kicked it into first, hit the start button, grabbed plenty of throttle and we roared off. Behind me, Caitlin jerked back like a rag doll. I thought she was going to fall off, but she clamped her arms around me and we sped up the bank in a blaze of torchlight. Black Death lifted off as we crested the bank. Then landed perfectly, and we raced on the path towards the car park. Again, we were bathed in light. This time from the front. More Police were coming in the direction of the car park. Dipping my shoulder, I leant over to the left and steered the VFR off the path and into the dark woods. Branches whipped my face. I put my hand up to stop them, but I couldn't ride one handed. It was hard enough using both hands to keep us upright. I flipped on the light switch; at least I might see them coming. Chucking the bike this way, and that, navigating through the low trees and bushes, Caitlin was being tossed all over the place. She still seemed to be enjoying herself though. Every now, and again I could hear her breaking into fits of laughter. To be honest, I was beginning to enjoy myself too, that is, until a copper stepped out in front of us, blinding us with his torch. He put his hand up instructing us to stop like it was a main road. I thought, fuck off, cunt, and gave it some throttle and rode straight at him. He dived out of the way into the mud. Caitlin screeched with delight, and I couldn't help laughing too. I carried on riding for what felt like ages until I felt Caitlin hitting my back. I cocked my head, trying to hear her,

"What? What is it?"

"OK, it's OK, we've lost them. Pull over, pull over," she insisted, driving her left foot forward seeking out the brake pedal.

Exhaling, I sat upright, loosened my grip on the throttle and let the bike slow down, using dynamic braking. She was right. There were no lights anywhere around us. The clunch pit must have been a couple of miles behind us at least. I stopped next to an old oak tree and jumped off laughing. She rushed up and rammed me up against the tree. To start with I thought she was attacking me, then she plunged her tongue into my mouth and started tugging at my belt. I felt my cock hardening, there was no way I was going to stop her; my anticipation had wiped out any past animosity. I ran my hands over her small firm breasts and gently pinched her erect nipples. She moaned softly, then dropped to her knees, pulling down my trousers. She put my cock in her mouth and threw her head backwards and forwards viciously. Now and again, she ran her teeth down my shaft, making me flinch then feeling my discomfort, it would be back to those beautiful, yielding lips. Leaning back against the gnarly bark of the tree, I looked up at the shimmering moon. Bestial feelings rose up within me. I wanted to howl. She pulled away, then lay down on the ground and wriggled out of her denim skirt, revealing her creamy white skin. Throwing the rest of my clothes off, I dropped down. She smiled at me as I went to get on top of her, then at the last second, she spun me over and climbed on top. I snorted, pushed my cock up. Then she spat on her hand, grabbed my cock rubbing it up and down, then lowered herself, easing onto it. Both of us gasped as she began to move up and down. To start with I helped her by gripping her thighs, bearing some of the weight, but as she picked up speed, I realised she didn't need any. Her rhythm was intoxicating, irresistible. There was nothing else I could do but lie back and enjoy the ride. Soon both of us were panting like dogs, drawing in deep breaths of air. Breathless, I looked up at her silhouette framed on the ghostly background. I had to have her lips on mine, so I put my hands on her shoulders and drew her to me, but something rubbed on my belly. There was something in the way. I peered down. It was the Den bump. That fucking little alien was between us again. My mind began to race. Images of Den's stupid gormless face flooded in. His food encrusted beard, his red slitted eyes, his greasy hair. His self-deluded comeback of, 'on my kid's eyes' when he was lying came back to me. Then, horror of horrors. I saw the alien, the alien cocooned inside Caitlin's belly with Den's features, my cock battering it, whacking its forehead. It was on his kid's fucking eyes now alright, I thought. No matter what I tried to think of, to shake it off, I couldn't. My stupid overactive imagination was beating my lust, hands down. Down below, I began to lose it. Caitlin felt she was losing me, so she upped the pace, leant forward, pressed her lips onto mine and pushed her tongue into my mouth. No doubt, I wanted it to be there again, find the essence, it was so beautiful, but I was trapped in that junkie bastard's labyrinth.

Caitlin sought out my ear and whispered, "Let me know when you're going to cum, I want you to cum in my mouth."

Den's face vanished. Blood flowed filling the void, Caitlin gasped, and I began to buck from below, thrusting upwards for all I was worth.

A couple of minutes of pure ecstasy later, I couldn't hold on any longer, "I'm going to cum now," I groaned.

Caitlin sniggered, then ducked down to my midriff, and wanked me off into her mouth. Breathing hard I came with everything I had. She gagged, threw her head back gargling, laughed, then spat out my cum onto the oak tree.

Staggering to my feet, I said, "That was fucking brilliant. Look, my legs are shaking; I think I've blown a fuse."

Now it was irresistible, I howled up at the luminescent moon, and she burst into laughter and joined in, shrieking at the top of her voice. Our calls echoed around the ghostly woods.

"I feel so alive when I'm with you Skinner," she told me, pulling her skirt on.

"Yeah? You're not bad yourself," I laughed.

"I can be myself with you, I feel free, so free. I want to be with you, always," she said, piercing me with her eyes.

"You're just drunk," I scoffed, backing away from her.

"I'm not... Well maybe a little, but I really mean it."

"Yeah?" I replied, busying myself pulling my Rukkas from my top box, hoping that she would look away. I didn't know what to say to that.

Adding the waterproofs to our clothes scattered on the ground, I made a bed for us.

Caitlin hugged me, "You're such a gentleman. You'd look after us, wouldn't you?"

Bowing low, I gestured for her to make herself comfortable,

"Right you are, your ladyship."

In that moment, humour was all I had; I couldn't answer that question without thinking over its connotations. Caitlin gave me a beaming smile, then we lay down together, folding ourselves around one another, sharing our warmth. Both of us became silent, looking up through the branches of the mighty oak tree at the ethereal glow of the moon. Pale and illuminating with its skull-like features, its eerie presence made me feel like there was someone else there, guiding us. It was surreal, the whole day had been. From the pig's carcass, to Geraldine, to HMV, to the drop in Horley. Now this. What was I supposed to make of this? I didn't know. Caitlin had made a fool of me once already, and I had sworn to myself that she would never do it again, but I couldn't help myself. She was an amazing woman. She was totally fucking crazy. I started thinking about what it would be like to live with her, the fun we would have, and of course being Natty's stepdad. Natty was such a bright ray of sunlight in an often cold and unforgiving world. In her company I felt good, felt like I was doing something positive, even noble. With her about I could see there was more to life than chaos and debauchery. Bearing that in mind, maybe Den's baby wouldn't be a problem after all. Nature was all powerful, but nurture could change everything. Why couldn't I bring up Den's baby as my own? I would be a better dad than that bastard could ever be. If the cunt got in our way, I'd fucking knock him out, put him in hospital. If he took us to court, trying to get custody, a smackhead like him would have no chance. There'd only be one winner and that would be Caitlin. I inhaled deeply, glanced at her staring up at the luminescent sky, trying to think what was going on beneath the surface. What was she thinking? Obviously, she'd enjoyed herself tonight, but did it really mean anything, or was she just hedging her bets like the last time? Or maybe she was just pissed up, talking shit and going to regret what she said in the morning? I didn't know. I'm not sure she did either, after all, we were just two people trying to find a way through the maze.

NO ONE IS INNOCENT.

In the small hours of the morning, I crawled out of bed, dressed quietly and snuck downstairs to the kitchen. Opening the fridge door, I seized a couple of last night's unwanted sausages and stuck them in a bag. Tiptoeing, I made my way to the front door, undid the latch and crept out into the twilight. Keeping my eyes peeled, scouring Longwood Road for any signs of life, I made my way up to the junction with the Ridgeway. I'm not sure why I was being so furtive, because the only person I didn't want to see was Kipper. Renny had told me that he had locked Stink in a shed around his back garden. He had also assured me that Tracy had taken a shine to the terrier and was feeding him regularly, but just in case, I bought the sausages along. Coming up to Kipper's block, I tensed up. Surely the fat bastard would still be sleeping, I thought. Everybody else was. Navigating my way through the wind-blown washing lines at the back of his block, I came to the small garden. Even in the early morning light it was clear the place was in a right old state. It looked like all the junk that had been in the kitchen before Kipper's return had been tossed out into the garden. There were rusty old pots and pans, broken chairs and a table piled up in readiness for a fire. Set back from the pyre was what I can only describe as a cage. Renny had been well off, a shed would've been luxury compared to this. It was about the size of a milk crate. Nobody was about, but if anyone happened to look out of the window, I would stick out like a sore thumb, so I got down on all fours. Peeping up at the blind windows, I crawled up to the low chain link fence that marked the boundary of the shit heap. Expecting Stink to start barking at any moment, I drew one of the sausages out of the bag in readiness. I called him a couple of times, keeping my voice low but there was still nothing. There was no way he couldn't have heard me. He was an amazing guard dog. In one swift motion, I hopped over the low fence and got back down onto all fours again, still watching those windows.

"Stink? Stink, are you there boy?" I implored taking it up a notch.

Nothing, still nothing. It didn't bode well. I knew him. If there was anything about, he'd always start yapping, going mad, warning everybody. Crawling low, through the dirty grass, I came to the cage, I whispered again, and the white patches of his face appeared.

"Stink! You alright boy? It's me."

Tentatively he edged forward and sniffed my fingers, then recognising my scent, he began nuzzling my hand through the holes in the wire.

"Stink, oh mate, how are you?" I said, tickling above his eyes, but when I moved to the top of his head, he whimpered.

"What is it mate? What's up?" I said, gently running my hand through his hair.

Stink wasn't the most fastidious of dogs at the best of times, but something was up; his hair was matted, stuck together. Between my forefinger and thumb, I squeezed a matted tuft. It became sticky. Even though it was dark, and I couldn't see, I knew straightaway what it was. It was blood. A lot of blood. He'd obviously taken a proper fucking hiding.

"Jesus, fucking Christ," I hissed.

Scowling up at the window, I took one of the sausages from my bag, "Here boy, look," I whispered pushing it through the grill.

He swallowed it in one, then he did the same with the other. He was starving hungry. I didn't know what to do. There was no way I could leave him. Not like that.

"It's OK boy. I'm going to get you out of here," I told him, reaching for the bolt.

Wrenching it sideways, I found it didn't move. It was stuck tight. Then I saw the padlock hanging down. My heart sank. I sighed, thinking, even if I get him out, what am I going to do with him? If I take him back to the flat, it wouldn't take Kipper long to find out what had happened. He has eyes all over the estate. Nah, it's way too dangerous. I'm going to have to leave him, try and think of a way I can do this properly. Because if I get it wrong, it's going to be bad for both of us. Stink looked up at me expectantly, waiting for me to let him out.

"I'm sorry. It's locked mate, I can't do anything."

I scratched him for a while longer, then I got up onto my haunches, "I'll be back boy, I promise I'll be back, just hang in there," I told him, backing away.

Stink pushed forwards against the mesh trying to follow.

I whispered, "I'm sorry mate. I'll save you, you'll see," and with one final glance, I was off.

On my way back down the Ridgeway, my mind was in turmoil. I felt like a right cunt leaving him behind, locked up in that condition. I felt sick. Everybody knew what was going on, but nobody was doing anything about it because of Kipper. The bloke was a Class A cunt. I thought, the next time he fucks with me, I'm going to fucking do him, but I was only fooling myself. He'd grind me to ash with one hand tied behind his back. By the time I got back to my yard, the first rays of the sun were forming skeletal shapes under the washing lines, and I was beginning to calm down. The way I was feeling, I needed to. The last thing I wanted was to wake anyone up in the flat because there would be the inevitable questions. Inevitable questions, I didn't have answers for. Carefully unlocking the door, I noticed there was a light on in the kitchen. It wasn't the main light. It looked like it was coming from the fridge. Briefly I wondered if I had left it open on my way out. Sneaking into the hallway, I stopped. Den stood unsteadily, rooting around in the fridge, looking for something to eat. He was off his nut.

"Boo," I said to the dopey twat, shouldering my way in.

"Bloody hell Skinner. Don't do that, you almost gave me a heart attack," he parried, switching back on, putting his hand on his chest to illustrate.

"You just getting in?" He grinned, picking up an old tomato, turning it over, examining it.

"Something like that."

He smiled knowingly, "I had a big night last night myself. I'm done in. I can't do it like I used to."

Yeah, I thought, a big night smacked out, lying on Aiden's floor? You degenerate cunt.

Den discarded the tomato in the crammed sink,

"This place is a dump," he muttered.

From upstairs, we heard Natty crying.

Den rolled his eyes, "Here we go, the little bitch is looking for attention again."

Immediately balling my fists, "What did you say?" I demanded.

"Yeah, well," he bleated, backing off, "I'm just having a moan. I didn't mean nothing by it."

"She's a bright little girl; you should look after her. And Caitlin," I raged.

Den scrutinised me, he might have been an idiot, but he wasn't fucking stupid, "What's this all about? You trying to get in with Caitlin?"

"No. But you wouldn't give a shit, even if I was," I seethed as my parting shot, turning to leave.

Den smiled contemptuously, "Help yourself Skinner, you'd be doing me a favour."

Nothing was the best thing to say to him, especially when he was out of it, but I still called him a 'cunt', under my breath. Then I went up to my bedroom, feeling the need to get some more sleep. Before I got back into bed, paranoia took over and I checked my record collection. Everything was in order, present and correct, but I noticed my guitar had been moved again. I was thinking of going back down and having it out with the bastard, but I knew it would be a waste of time. He would just deny it like he always did. A few hours later, I woke up feeling hungry, so I went downstairs to the kitchen, hoping that Den wasn't about. If he started going on about my little show of emotion in front of Caitlin or worse still Natty, it would be embarrassing for all of us and leave me with only one option: to knock him out. Caitlin and me getting together had been on my mind since the night at the clunch pit. Even though we'd had crazy off this planet sex a couple of times, since then, I still hadn't made my mind up about her. I wanted to go for it, but there was something in the back of my mind telling me to be careful, hold back. Den wasn't about, so I made myself some breakfast, took it into the front room, and sat down with Pete to watch the TV. It was the news. I hated the fucking news. It was always the same bullshit, designed to frighten the masses, to keep them insecure and running around on the hamster wheel. Normally I'd ignore it, but today, they were actually saying something which was of some interest to me. Weatherman Michael Fish was being interviewed about a possible hurricane coming to the U.K. Despite all the evidence, the weatherman was adamant. There was nothing to worry about; there was no hurricane.

"Well, thank fuck for that," I said chomping down on a piece of toast, "I wouldn't want to ride a bike in a hurricane."

Pete nodded thoughtfully; he was already stoned. I liked a smoke as much as anybody else did, but at this time of the morning, I just wanted to wake up, find something to do, achieve something. No matter how small. Fuck knows what I was going to achieve today though. There was nothing going on. I thought if nothing happens by midday, then I may as well join Pete, have a few smokes, chillout before going back to the madhouse tomorrow.

Natty barged the door open, "Skinner who is Cerys?"

"What? How do you know her?"

"She sent you a letter," she told me, holding up a handful of letters.

Pete dragged his red eyes away from the vivid TV lights, "Oooooh, is this the infamous Cerys?" He enquired.

"Now, let's see what we've got here," I said ignoring him, taking the letters from Natty.

"It's the one with the pretty picture, Skinner," pointed Natty.

"Oh, it's a postcard, nice one," I announced, keeping my voice neutral.

If they thought I was going to read it in front of them, they had another thought coming, so I stashed it in my back pocket and then flipped through the others.

Taking three out of the bunch, I handed the rest to Pete, "Here you go Pete, if you can just file them, please," I sniggered, passing over the final reminders.

Pete cracked up, "Only three today," he said, tossing them into the wastepaper bin at his side.

Natty smiled, peered at us, then at the bin again, "Are you two being naughty?" she asked.

Pete laughed, "No, they were wrong addresses."

I stifled a laugh. "So what are you doing today Natty?"

"Don't know, mummy said we might go to the park later."

"I'm not doing anything this morning; shall we get my guitar down?"

Natty's head dropped, and she trudged out, shaking her head slowly from side to side, "No, no guitar. I don't like guitar."

Pete said, "You've got a real way with kids you have Skinner," grinning at my puzzled face.

"Oh well," I said standing up.

I made my way into the kitchen and retrieved the postcard from my pocket and read:

Hello from sunny Italy,
I'm in Venice now. I can't believe I'm here, it's been brilliant, but this is my last cruise.
All good things must come to an end I suppose... I'm coming home next month, and I'm having a party at Millfield. Please come, it would be great to catch up.
Hope all is well with you.
Love Cerys xxx.

Caitlin strode into the kitchen, and I hid the postcard like I was doing something wrong.

Natty breezed in behind her, singing, "Skinner's got a girlfriend! Mummy, he got a letter from her, didn't you Skinner?"

Caitlin stared at me, waiting for me to say something, but I didn't. I just held her gaze.

"You shouldn't read other people's mail, Natty," she scolded her daughter.

"No, it's OK. It was a postcard. She's just an old friend."

She shook her head, "Well, I think you should say sorry Natty, that's very naughty."

"No, it's fine," I exhaled.

"Well?" Ignoring me, glaring at Natty.

"I'm, I'm, sorry, Skinner," she said, tears welling up in her eyes.

"You've been horrible to Skinner; he asked you if you wanted to play guitar. I heard you saying no, you're always saying no. Stop being horrible, go and play guitar."

Natty started crying.

Caitlin's reaction had been well over the top, totally unnecessary, I didn't know where her head was at. Natty was in a right state, I thought maybe she needed a break, so I crouched down.

"Come on Natty, let's leave mummy to do all these horrible dirty dishes. Let's go and have some fun, shall we?" I said, gently taking her hand.

Nodding solemnly, she gave me the thinnest of smiles, while Caitlin just glowered at us. She then turned to the sink and began washing up noisily, chucking stuff about, so we left her to it.

Pete got himself out of his chair when he saw me and Natty come in with my flying V.

He said, "There's a storm coming Skinner. And you best be ready when she does."

Cracking up, I actually thought he was talking about Caitlin for a moment, then I heard the telly. They were still going on about a hurricane. I must admit it was pretty windy outside, but it was no worse than the start of October.

"Yeah, well we've got more important things to do now, haven't we Natty," I smiled, strumming the flying V.

Natty just stared into space.

Pete gave her an uncertain look, "OK, OK, I'm going," he grumbled, already on his heels.

"Me and Brandon are going up the Griffin, if you want to join us later? The more the merrier."

"Nah, you're alright, not with Kipper there," I told him, plugging the V into my amplifier.

"Oh, he's alright... The last time I was up there he was buying drinks for everyone," he told me before closing the door.

For fucks sake, I thought, the fat bastard is after hearts and minds now, well he's not getting mine, the Nazi asshole. No sooner had I set everything up, I beckoned Natty to come over and sit on my knee like we used to, but she shook her head from side to side.

"Don't want to."

"Come on Natty I won't bite you," I said laughing, then I clamped my jaws together and made a roaring sound.

Natty laughed and growled back.

"Come on we haven't played in ages, I've been missing it," I told her truthfully.

Natty giggled, hopped up on my knee and the guitar lesson began. I went back over the chords I had taught her at the beginning of our lessons. It had been a while, so I thought she'd have forgotten them, but no. E, D and A chords were no problem at all. Not just a little surprised, I decided to move on, find something more challenging for her. I showed her the C chord, which is a real stretch for your fingers to start with. She did it. No problem. I couldn't believe it; it had taken me weeks to stretch my fingers like that. I started feeling suspicious. Maybe Den hadn't been in my room messing with my guitar after all, maybe it had been Natty.

"Do you know F?"

Natty smiled shyly. "Yes, and I know the P chord too."

"There is no P chord, Natty," I snorted.

She giggled, "Yes there is, look," she said and put her hand between my legs and squeezed my crotch.

My hand shot down and swatted it away, "What are you doing?"

She slumped forward, her bottom lip jutted out, "It's the P …"

"Don't do that, what the…" I didn't have time to finish because she leapt off me and ran for the door, crying.

A few moments later, the door crashed open, and Caitlin raced in, "What did you do to her?" She demanded menacingly.

I said, "I don't know, she just..."

"She just what?" She continued, her voice rising.

There was no way I was going to tell her what happened. I couldn't. Even though I hadn't done anything, I felt ashamed.

"She just, she just started crying, OK? She's always crying these days."

"And that's my fault, is it?" She bellowed.

"No of course it's not."

"Listen Skinner, you don't want to mess with me. Kipper hates me and I hate him, but one word from me and you're in big trouble."

Enough was enough, I got up, pushed past her, and made my way into the kitchen and stood by the window, staring out into the yards. I needed to get out. Get out, before I said something to Caitlin I would regret. In amongst feelings of shame, and confusion, I felt like I'd been wronged, attacked for no reason. It wasn't my fucking fault. I didn't do anything wrong. All I was doing was trying to help out, make Natty's life better... And now this. Forcing it down, I decided there was only one person I could talk to about this, and that was Mia. She would understand, she'd know what to do. I could ride up to her place in Cambridgeshire, be there within the hour. Picking up the phone, I dialled her number and waited.

"Hello?" A bloke's voice.

"Oh, hi Mr. Knight, is Mia there?"

"Who is this?"

"It's Skinner, I don't know if you remember me."

"I remember you all right. You're a cunt."

Now I was confused, I'd only met Mia's old man once, he was alright, and it seemed like he thought I was alright too. This wasn't Mia's old man.

"Who the fuck are you?"

"Never mind who I am, if you phone Mia again, you're fucking dead."

Then I knew who it was, it was Savy, Mia's old boyfriend. A few years earlier, Renny and me had some aggro with Savy and his band *Savage Circle,* ending with us wrecking their tour bus. The truth was, I didn't know that they'd got back together again, but I wasn't going to take any shit from the egotistical little bastard.

"How's your tour bus dickhead?" I taunted.

"You and your faggot mates are fucking dead," he shouted, and the line went dead.

"Yeah, you too," I shouted back to no one.

Caitlin's head appeared around the door. "What's happened? Are you OK?" She ventured, using a more conciliatory tone.

"It's nothing," I said dismissively.

"Sounded like something to me," she shifted uncomfortably, "look, I'm sorry you're right. Natty does cry a lot. I'm going out of my mind with worry about her, and there's Den and the baby," she said, her voice cracking.

Exhaling, I took her in my arms, "It's all going to be OK, don't worry," I said softly.

The Den bump pressed against me, keeping us apart, I deflated inwardly.

"What is it Skinner?" She replied, feeling my resistance.

No matter what we did, wherever we went, when we did it, there would always be the fucking Den bump, whether it was in nappies or in the womb. But at that moment her grip was so strong, so in need of a human touch, that I pushed it out of my mind. She pulled back, her soft breath was on my cheek, I turned to her. Then just like a clichéd TV soap, the phone rang.

She rolled her eyes, picked it up, "Hello?"

"Oh right," she said, "It's Mia," tossing the phone at me.

"Hi Mia," I said watching her march out.

"Well done, Skinner, you're a right idiot do you know that? They're coming down, they've got baseball bats and they're coming down, so well done."

"Who's coming down Mia?" I countered, genuinely not knowing what she was going on about.

"Savy, Sulli and the rest of *Savage Circle,*" she bristled, her temper rising.

"They're wankers."

"Yeah, yeah, everybody's a wanker. He's a wanker. They're wankers. It's always the same with you. You're just a magnet for trouble. You love it don't you? Well, I fucking don't. Don't phone me again," and that was it, she was gone.

Caitlin glowered at me as I retreated into the hallway with my tail between my legs; the bullshit was getting worse by the second. I thought fuck this, I'm going up the Griffin to have a couple of pints with Pete. He's got the right idea. Oblivion. I snatched my leather jacket from the coat stand and left the flat, slamming the door off its hinges on the way out. The wind hit me as soon as I left the shelter of the yards. The way it was, I thought there might be a hurricane coming after all. Everything was being tossed in the air. Head down, bending forwards, I made my way up Longwood Road and onto the Ridgeway towards the pub. Lunchtimes were busy at the Golden Griffin and today was no exception, the car park was full. In amongst the knackered-out cars owned by the Farm's residence, I noticed Renny's BMW parked up in front of the fire exit where he usually parked it. He must've picked up Alice. I shoved the thick dark wooden door open, and the blustery wind subsided. In the corner of the saloon bar, at the head of the table that was used for lunches, sat Kipper. Aiden, Ridsey, Shads and another six or seven other blokes I'd never seen before, sat with him. Then I looked again. One of them was Jace, the bloke I'd hit with a rolling pin when he'd tried to steal herb from me a few years earlier. Kipper looked up, muttered something, and the heads turned as one in my direction. I was thinking of leaving, when Renny and Alice waved to me from the main bar, so ignoring the looks from Kipper's Kaos Krew, I wandered over to greet them.

"What are you doing in the pub this early Skinner? I thought you liked to achieve something before you got mashed?" He said, taking the piss.

"What was that you said? Fuck the whole world for today?"

"Oh yeah, well it's like that sometimes."

I nodded thoughtfully.

Renny bought me a pint and I sipped at it, trying to listen to their easy uncomplicated conversation, but my mind kept returning to Natty. What the fuck was that all about? I just couldn't get my head around it. Why had she done that? Whatever the reason, I felt shame. Deep shame. Fuck knows why, but I couldn't help it. Something had happened to her, and I'd missed it. Den. Fucking Den. But surely me or Caitlin would've seen something.

"What's up with you Skinner?"

Not knowing enough myself, I decided to tell him, about the phone call with Savy, and the threats he made about coming down to the Farm and fucking us all up.

"You reckon he was serious?"

"I don't know, they came down before. Didn't they?"

Renny nodded, rubbing his thumb on the outside of his pint glass, "Yeah, it was lucky we weren't about," he told Alice, smiling.

"Oh alright, Kipper?" he said, casually looking up.

"Sunday drinking, I couldn't be happier."

Kipper's eyes fixed on me, "What you doing in my pub Skinner? There's no dogs allowed, son," he taunted me.

Seeing the look on my face, he sneered, "Look at him, he's shitting it Renny."

Renny pulled a smile, "He is."

Kipper nodded, "I'm only pulling your pisser, do you want a pint?"

"Y, yeah nice one, cheers," I muttered.

"You know where the bar is dear," he grinned and disappeared to the bogs.

Renny told me he was winding me up, he was doing it to everyone. 'Kip' had put fifty quid behind the bar, and I should take advantage of it and go get another drink. I thought OK, anything's better than going back to the flat now, and joined the scrum of people around the bar. Everyone was waving their 5- and 10-pound notes at the bar staff, who were doing their best to serve everyone, but I was getting nowhere. I was knocked forward by a hand coming down hard on my shoulder. Next to me Kipper was grinning,

"You need to wave some money at them son, that's the only way you'll get their attention," he said, holding out a £50 note, "Go on wave it, see what happens."

Kipper saw I wasn't going to take it, he tutted and called out, "Oi Reg, when you're ready mate."

Reg left a pint of lager under the tap and nodded at Kipper.

"Pint of lager for me and a snakebite for young Skinner here, Reg." Kipper smiled.

Reg quickly sorted him out and then got back to the overflowing pint glass under the tap.

As we jostled our way from the bar Kipper said, "Come around Lenny's later, there's sleeves of cigarettes and pouches of bacci, that need outing, you can make some big money."

"Yeah, OK, I will, cheers," I nodded, thinking I'd rather fucking die you cunt.

Kipper smirked and disappeared into the saloon bar while I headed back to my bar stool.

Easing myself down, I sipped my pint. It didn't taste good; it tasted like surrender.

Renny and Alice watched me intently then finally Renny said, "What was that about?"

"He wants me to knock out some smokes for him."

"Well, are you?"

"No fucking chance. Nazis cunts fuck off."

Renny exhaled deeply, looked to Alice and shook his head.

Alice said, "Come on you two, forget him, it's drinking time."

Renny and me exchanged a grin, then we nodded at Alice; we may not have agreed on how to handle Kipper's return, but we knew a good idea when we heard it. A few pints later, the world looked a lot better, and with Alice up at the bar getting her round in, it was about to get better still. Sitting back waiting, I looked out of the window towards the shops on Tudor Way and watched a group of motorcyclists ride into the car park. There wasn't anything particularly powerful amongst them, just your everyday low powered bikes, but I recognised the CM 250 because Nev at Central Express had one. They stopped and began to dismount. One of them lifted off his crash helmet. I couldn't believe my eyes, it was Sulli. Then next to him, Savy took off his. They exchanged a few words, then Savy strutted into the newsagent.

"Renny, look," I said, but he had already seen and was watching intently.

"I think we should go and say hello. What do you think?" He said.

Every bit of angst I'd felt that day rose up inside me. I was drowning in it. It was a poisonous bile, that had to be exorcised. Exorcised on these fuckers. Nodding, I got up and followed him outside. I was buzzing, ready for a scrap as we shouldered up to them, but as soon as they saw Renny coming at them, they jumped back on their bikes and sped off into the Farm.

"Shitters," exclaimed Renny, "Come on, we'll get them," he shouted, already running.

Renny dived into his car, started it up, while I piled into the shotgun seat, then wheels spinning, we left the car park and headed into the Farm ourselves. By driving into the Farm, they'd fucked themselves. Fucked themselves good and proper, because there was only one way in and out. It was only a matter of time until we caught up with them. Renny did a quick circuit of the north part of the estate, then he parked up in a row of cars, on Welwyn Road, just down from the only exit. Not long after, the bikes appeared at the top of Tudor Way and took a right turn. It couldn't have worked out any better. Renny started the motor just as the last of them went past, then he hit the accelerator, and we were right on its tail. The rider's head turned in surprise. Then he swerved left and right, trying to stop us coming up next to him. He had no chance. Renny waited for his moment, then as the bike swerved to the left, he dropped the BMW from 4th to 3rd and shot up on his outside. He then cut in. The bike began to wobble. The panicking rider's head spun around. I opened the BM's heavy door, smacking it onto the side of the bike. The bike veered left, hit the pavement and chucked the rider off onto the grass verge. Renny hit the brakes, and we came to a screeching halt. I jumped out, ran to the sprawling rider, kicking him hard in the ribs. He shouted and ripped off his crash helmet. I was hoping it was Savy, I wanted to smack that cunt one, but it was Sulli. Sulli was alright, he had fucked me around with my band a few years earlier, but that was it. I didn't want to hurt him.

Renny had other ideas though, he ran up behind me and said, "Fucking hit him, Skinner. What you waiting for?"

Sulli backed off with his hands up, looking left and right for somewhere to run, but there was nowhere.

"Please, Skinner, come on, please no," he pleaded.

"Fucking do him, Skinner," insisted Renny.

"Please I only came for the ride. Savy wanted to brick your windows. I told him not to!"

I smashed him on the nose, pushing through with all my body weight, and he fell backwards onto the ground.

"Don't fucking come back here again do you hear me?" I told him.

"I won't honest, I won't," he snivelled, slowly getting back to his feet.

Renny snarled, "Finish him off."

"I have finished him off. He's done, man, fucking done."

Renny snorted, "No, he's fucking not, he's standing, he came here with his mates to fuck you up, and you're going to hit him once and that's it?"

"Please," he begged.

"He's done; it's over Renny."

"Bollocks, is he, do him."

Suddenly I was on the floor. I looked up and saw Kipper tromping past, raging. He hit Sulli with a volley of shots to the face and he went down onto the ground, then Kipper closed in and started kicking him. Sulli screamed, begging for mercy, but there was none coming. Kipper just kept on kicking and kicking and kicking until the sweat was dripping off his red face.

"This is how it's done, Skinner, watch, watch and learn you fucking clown," he shouted, as his DM boots smashed down onto the helpless Sulli.

"Please," whispered Sulli, from somewhere far away.

"That's enough, come on. He's had enough," I begged.

Kipper rounded on me and elbowed me back down, "You're not going to start crying again like you did with that fucking mutt, are you?"

I said nothing.

"Fucking hell Renny, you soppy cunt. You reckon this piss stain stepped in for you at the 100 Club? What was it? Gay night?"

Aiden and Ridsey, emerging from behind, cracked up laughing in agreement.

"Let's go, before the filth show up. If you want help in the future Skinner? Here's a fuck off with a frame around it," Kipper laughed, still scrutinising Sulli.

Sulli sucked in air.

Kipper winked at his new audience, "More? You want more, boy? Here you go," he jeered stamping down on his head.

"Come on boys. See you later, dear," he said, pointing at me as he strolled off laughing with Aiden and Ridsey following close behind laughing.

Soon as they were out of earshot, I said, "Renny, we've got to get him to hospital, man."

He thought about it, then with a slow shake of his head, he turned and walked to his car.

"What the fuck are you doing? We can't leave him like this, we need to help him."

"He's not going anywhere in my car, if Kipper sees, I'll be fucked."

"For fuck's sake he could die. Please man, this isn't right. You know that."

Renny climbed in, "It's him or me, and I choose me," he shouted back and drove off.

RIDERS ON THE STORM.

On the way into work, I witnessed the havoc the storm had wreaked on the South East of England in the night. Everywhere, there were trees down. In the fields surrounding the A10, huge oaks and elms that had stood for hundreds of years lay prone, bowled over by the sheer force of the wind. The roads had fared no better. Near the turn off to Cheshunt, a tree had fallen blocking one side of the carriageway. In their desperation to get to work, drivers were crossing the muddy central reservation to bypass the obstacle. Further down the road from Cheshunt, near the Potters Bar roundabout, I rode past a high-backed Tesco lorry lying flat on its side, its cab window smashed and gaping like a screaming mouth. I wondered how long it would be until I saw another one. Not long afterwards, as I crossed the M25 bridge, there it was. Lying on its side, its container doors were open, and its load was strewn across the carriageways. Before I'd left the Farm that morning, I had thought that it would be impossible to ride on a day like this, but the going was pretty good to start with. In the open countryside, the wind was constant, and for the most part blowing in the same direction, so all I had to do was lean into it to stay upright. It was only when I got into the built-up areas north of London, that the problems started. In the towns the houses worked like windbreaks, keeping me sheltered, but every time there was a gap or a side road, the vicious crosswinds chucked me sideways. Keeping my wits about me, I tried to predict which way the wind was going to hit me from next, but it was impossible. It was coming from all angles. It was a fucking nightmare. I started thinking about turning back, going home, but I couldn't afford to. Work had been slow during the week, and I needed to do the full five days to qualify for my guarantee of £300. If I went home, I'd miss a day and only get my earnings which wasn't great - probably about £180. Expecting to hear Graham, I turned my radio on at the Roundway, but there seemed to be a dozen controllers on the same frequency, squelching each other out. Fuck knows what was going on. I knew one thing though: I was going to earn my money today. By the time I hit Holloway, the traffic was thinning. It was weird, I'd never seen it like that before. Not at this time of the day. Usually it was bumper-to-bumper all the way through Holloway down into the City, but it looked like the storm had put people off. They were staying at home, kicking back, taking it easy, waiting for it to blow over. It made sense to me. Finally reaching Domingo Street, I breathed a huge sigh of relief. It felt like I had been on a long journey, a long journey through an unfamiliar land. Hopping off Black Death, I saw there were only three bikes parked up on the double yellow lines outside Central Express. Noel's Suzuki, Yacob's BMW and Muttley's Honda C70. TNT's EC1 office was closed. It looked like Shirley hadn't made it in either, which was unusual for her. She was a proper trooper; she always made the effort to come in and she liked working late with Graham. Leaving the wind channelling down Domingo Street, I shut the door and tromped up the steep staircase to the rider's room on the first floor.

Noel greeted me with a fist bump as I sat down, taking the weight off. "Skinner, I can't believe you made it man," he said pulling off his glasses and pretending to clean them.

"I had no choice mate, I want that guarantee," I returned grinning at Muttley and Yacob who both had to be in for the same reason.

"I hear that, I got to get mine," he said, "I tell you man, that wind is crazy, it nearly had me on my backside."

Graham popped his head through the window of the radio room, greeting me, "Did anyone see the news this morning?"

Noel and me shook our heads.

"I've never seen such carnage in all my life, the hurricane has devastated this country."

Muttley nodded, "Yeah, it's blown down five of the oak trees at Sevenoaks."

"What are they going to call it now, Twooaks?" I asked.

Noel cracked up laughing, his dreads dancing chaotically. "Twooaks," he said, trying it out.

Graham laughed, "Doesn't have the same ring to it does it?"

"No, it is not so grand," agreed Yacob.

Muttley gave him a friendly shove, "I bet you'd still get all the jobs going there, you always get the distance work."

Yacob grinned, "Of course, I have a big bike, you have a shit bike."

Noel and me exchanged a glance; we loved it when they started.

"Mine could do Sevenoaks no problems," returned Muttley.

"In two weeks," replied Yacob.

Everyone cracked up.

"Ohhhh," intoned Noel.

"He's got you there," I said conclusively.

"OK, OK, come on" said Graham, putting his hand up for us to listen, "I've got good news and bad news. The bad news is that we only have four bikes today."

Nobody was laughing now.

"You haven't heard the good news yet," he said pausing for effect, "The good news is, well, from your point of view, the telephones aren't working. We've only got pre-books for this morning. Hopefully things will get better later."

"I knew I should've stayed in bed this morning," wailed Muttley, half-jokingly.

Yacob smiled, "But you must come in. You have to buy your CDs now."

Everyone cracked up.

"Borstal Breakout, by Sham 69, would be a good place to start," I grinned.

Everyone including Graham knew he had been nicked after our run in at HMV. I was surprised he hadn't been hospitalised after the whack he got on his head, but Muttley reckoned that he was made of stronger stuff. As for the law, he was up in court at the end of the month. Did it bother him? From what I saw, he couldn't give a fuck. Graham handed out the dockets for the pre-books and we wrote them down in our books, then we made our way outside. Now it was time to see what we were made of. Muttley got on his C70 and turned it over.

I cupped my ear, "Er, have you actually started that monstrosity?"

Yacob shook his head, "I can't hear anything."

"My sister's hairdryer is more powerful than that," Noel laughed.

"It is probably faster as well," quipped Yacob, pulling on his crash helmet.

"Oi, fuck off," said Muttley protectively covering the C70's twist grips, like they were its ears, "Clementine, would do all your bikes in the city, no sweat."

Noel snorted, "Yeah, yeah, we know. You'd use the pavements."

Muttley revved up his engine, making it scream, "I'd use the fucking lifts given half the chance."

Yacob raised his hand, smiled and smoothly rode off on his BMW.

"You looking for a burn up Skinner, man?" Invited Noel, revving his own.

"Nah, no way Noel, not in this weather mate, it's hard enough to stay upright as it is," I told him fastening the strap on my crash helmet.

"Who was that fucking weatherman that didn't see this coming?" I asked.

"Michael Fish?"

"Yeah, that's him."

"Michael Fish is a bumbaclot, man."

Nodding in agreement, I pressed the start button and watched the Rastafarian Carl Fogarty blast off down Domingo Street towards Fann Street. ICC Banner Street EC1, going W11 was my pre-book, which was perfect for me. There was a Video and Music Exchange shop opposite Notting Hill Gate tube station. If I was plotted up in the West end, not only would I have shelter, I'd be able to knock out the latest batch of half inched CDs from HMV. Black Death roared ominously underneath me. I let the clutch out and shot off up Domingo Street in a driving head wind. I turned right on Old Street, watching the mini tornadoes of newspapers and other accumulated rubbish from city life spewing up into the air. Banner Street was one-way, so I had to go around the back doubles to get to the top where ICC was. I parked up, picked up the parcel, then checking it on the way back to the VFR, I saw it was addressed to Ruby Wax. Considering I'd been working as a despatch rider for over five years; I hadn't done many drops for well-known people. Simon Mayo, Nick Cave, Boy George and Craig Charles. None of them were particularly pleasant or interesting experiences. Nick Cave was smacked out of his nut. Simon Mayo had been a complete wanker, and Boy George had been downright creepy; I'd never had a bloke come onto me before. Out of them all, Craig Charles was probably the worst though. It was such a disappointment. *Red Dwarf* had been one of my favourite TV shows when I was living at home. Mum and me used to watch it; it had brought us together. Lister was a character we could really relate to. He was funny, easy going and a bit of a rebel. Craig Charles did an amazing job bringing him to life, so I was excited when I read his name on one of my drops. The address was off Lambeth Walk, so I had no trouble finding it. Knocking on the door, I couldn't help but smile. I was about to meet my hero Listy, but it wasn't Listy who answered the door, it was a young pregnant woman. I handed her the letter and cheekily asked if Craig was about. She started crying. She told me, 'He wasn't in,' 'she didn't know where he was, or when he was coming back, if at all'. I was gobsmacked, I didn't know what to say, and before I could think of anything, she grabbed me and started sobbing on my shoulder. For the life of me I didn't know what to do. Then finally, after she'd cried herself out, she apologised and slammed the door in my face. I rode away thinking, what a bastard. I hoped that the Ruby Wax drop would turn out better, as I dropped her parcel into my newspaper bag. For the most part, I'd use the side stand when parking up, but with the way the wind was, I had to use the centre. I hauled Black Death forward, started up and took off down Banner Street at speed. Then as I came through the junction with Whitecross Street, I was knocked sideways by a brutal crosswind. Ducking down onto the tank, I leant hard into it, straightened up, but once I'd crossed the junction, the houses blocked the wind, and the resistance was gone. The tarmac rose up to meet me, so I threw my weight to the other side and straightened up again. On Old Street, I fared little better. Every time I went through a junction, I was hit by the crosswind. It became a bit of a game, until I came to the one between Clerkenwell Road and Farringdon Road. The wind was so powerful it threw me headlong in front of a speeding black cab. Furiously pumping his horn, the driver swerved, bounced up the kerb, narrowly avoiding a pedestrian. The game was over. Once I had got into W1, I was hoping the conditions would improve, but as it turned out it was just blind optimism. If anything, they got worse. The storm had hit the West End hard. Nearly every tree had been blown over, some of the bigger ones had landed on cars, crushing them under their huge boughs. Oxford Street was an absolute shambles. Keep left signs tumbled edge over edge, signs for roadworks clattered on concrete, while all manner of smaller objects; newspapers, cans, bottles, and discarded food containers, were tossed into the air. Everything that wasn't made of brick and mortar or bolted down was being chucked around chaotically. On the approach to Oxford Circus, I changed down to a lower gear in anticipation of the ferocious crosswind. Keeping myself low, I shot out into the junction. Before I'd made it across, a jagged piece of 'No Entry' sign span at me like a frisbee. I dodged sideways, but I was too slow; it bounced off my shoulder and disappeared into the circling maelstrom. Further along Oxford Street, near HMV, mountains of split boards and galvanised steel poles lay from downed scaffolding, some of it in the way. Nothing was stopping me though; a quick drop of my shoulder and I left the ruins in my rearview mirror. Even though it was early, the traffic at Marble Arch was thinning out. There were only about a dozen cars and a Red London bus on the roundabout, so I eased through with no problems. By the time I got halfway up the Bayswater Road, the traffic had all but disappeared. That, combined with a constant yet steady crosswind from the open expanse of Hyde Park, meant that the riding conditions improved considerably. Black Death sliced through the even wind, up to Notting Hill Gate, where I stopped at the red light. Checking to see if the Music and Video Exchange was open, I turned my head right. It was, good, I thought. Then I turned my attention back to the traffic lights. They were still red. A few minutes later, the light still hadn't changed. Noticing that the traffic coming in from Kensington Park Road hadn't moved either, I thought, the traffic lights must be stuck, so I ran the light and shot up Kensington Park Road. Soon, I had found the address. It was in a small muse near Portobello Market. I rolled to a stop, jumped off and made my way up to the posh studio flat. Tapping on the red door, I edged back a bit. I'd seen Ruby Wax on TV a few times. The truth was, I found her scary.

 Jennifer Saunders appeared in the doorway, giggling, "Oooooh, it's a biker," she called back into the flat.

Even though she'd played a girl called Helen Mucus in *The Young Ones,* I'd always had a thing about Jennifer Saunders, especially after a certain scene in *The Supergrass.* She was even better in the flesh, and she was well stoned. Nervously I handed her the package, feeling starstruck and not just a little bit horny. She gave me a massive smile.

"Thank you," she gushed, "And would you like me to sign somewhere?"

Ruby Wax stumbled into the hallway behind her and said, "Oh, wow, he's cute."

Jennifer laughed, "Yes, he is, very," she said, taking my docket book, brushing my hand.

I was glad of my crash helmet because I was going red. Docket book signed, she handed it back, watching my every move with amusement, "Must horrible out there?"

Nodding, I looked passed her into the warm flat.

"For God's sake Jennifer, shut the bloody door. You're letting a draft in," came a stern voice from inside.

She rolled her eyes, shrugged her shoulders, then gave me another big smile, "Bye, bye, biker, man, stay safe," she cooed and gently closed the door.

Exhaling, I wriggled my semi back to the right-hand side, and padded back to Black Death, thinking, maybe it's not such a bad day after all.

"Charlie, seven zero, seven zero," I called in into my radio.

There were still four or five controllers vying for supremacy of the frequency, but it was worth a try otherwise I would have to find a telephone box.

Low, and behold, Graham came back, "seven zero?"

"Empty, empty."

"Roger, Roger, seven zero, drift in, drift in."

"Roger, Rog," I said, letting the radio fall back onto my chest and started up.

Instead of going back the way I came, to avoid the wreckage of Oxford Street, I turned south, then took a left on Westbourne Grove and followed it onto Bishop Bridge Road. It was pretty much the same as it had been on the way: nasty crosswinds, fallen trees and swirling rubbish. Once I made it to Paddington, out of habit rather than anything else, I rode up the ramp to get onto the Marylebone Flyover. Even before I'd reached the top, I realised I'd made a serious mistake. Blasts of wind hit me full on, knocking me backwards on the saddle. Rain pelted my visor. There was no going back though, not on the ramp. So I carried on to the top, and looked for a gap in the speeding traffic. Elevated to this level, the wind increased tenfold, shoving the bike, tossing it left then right. It was impossible to control. I was totally powerless. Leaning forward on the tank, I tried to lower my resistance, but it was hopeless. There was nothing I could do. I was totally at the mercy of the elements. Cars swerved around me, blasting their horns. There was the hiss of hydraulic brakes. It was too much; I thought I was going to be hit at any moment. My hands began to shake. My nerve went completely. I couldn't take it anymore. So I moved over onto the hard shoulder, got my boots down onto the safely of the tarmac and stopped. Gasping in air, I took a moment. Then I slid along at 5 miles an hour, using my boots as stabilisers until thankfully the flyover's end came into view. On the downward slope, I switched back to the road, got a bit of speed up, and raced into Marylebone, where I found the traffic was backed up. Normally, even in the worst traffic jams cars would move. This was something different though. Nothing was moving. Everything had ground to a halt. It was gridlock. I began to weave the bulky road rocket around the static metal of cars, keeping an eye out for lane changers. Up ahead, there were flashing blue lights. There had been an accident at the

Eversholt Street junction. The road had been taped off. I weaved my way up to the tape and stopped. What I saw you could only describe as total carnage. There was a black cab wedged up on the central reservation, its windscreen smashed, the driver's door dented inwards. To the side of it lay a wrecked black Suzuki. Further down, the rider was flat out on the tarmac. As soon as I saw the dreadlocks, I knew who it was. Kicking the side stand, I jumped off, yanked the tape up and ran over to Noel. His eyes stared vacantly into space. Blood trickled from the corner of his mouth. I leant over him, put my hand on his chest,

"Jesus fucking Christ Noel, are you alright mate. Noel?"

Burst red lips moved trying to form words, trying to tell me something. Tell me something important, something I needed to hear. I put my ear to his mouth. "I beat him man, I beat him."

"What? Who? Who did you beat man?"

"The EXUP rider, I beat him, Skinner," he told me, proudly.

"Yeah, I bet you did mate. I bet you did," I returned, patting his shoulder.

Paramedics ushered me to one side, and I stood back watching while they worked on him, trying to save his life. Noel couldn't die, could he? I had only been talking to him that morning. He was young and strong like me. We didn't die. Old people died, not us.

"You need to move back please," a copper ordered, gesturing with his hands.

Giving him the briefest of nods, I made my way back to my bike and got on, still watching.

"Jesus fucking Christ," I muttered to no one.

Noel was given oxygen, carefully lifted onto a stretcher, and put into the back of the waiting ambulance. Watching the ambulance shoot off, snaking through the traffic, I grasped my radio,

"Charlie, seven zero, seven zero," I called.

"Seven zero?" replied Graham.

"Noel's come off and he's in a bad way. He's on the way to hospital."

"Roger that seven zero, we know, we know, go home seven zero, I repeat go home."

Signing off, I started up the VFR, and nipped across the pavement onto Eversholt Street, to start the long journey back to the Farm.

WAIT AND RETURN.

Considering how much damage the storm had caused across the country; it surprised me how little it had affected the Farm. A couple of felled trees and that was about it, and they'd been cleared away since I'd set off that morning. It was good to be back. I parked up in front of my yard, heaved off my crash helmet, scratched my matted scalp and breathed a huge sigh of relief. One day, that's all it was, but I felt like I'd been away for months. In fact, it felt like I'd been to the fucking moon and back. Pounding through the windswept yard, I noticed the clock in the neighbour's kitchen. It said 3.30pm. Good, I thought Den and Pete won't be about. I'll have a nice long soak in the bath and if Natty's at Caitlin's sister's, maybe Caitlin will join me. Unlocking the door, I pushed my way into the hall. There was music coming from the living room. It was my guitar. I would know it anywhere. If that's Den he's fucking dead, I thought, rushing in, but it wasn't. Natty was sitting on Aiden's knee playing, but as soon as she saw me, she jumped off and ran to the corner of the room. Aiden's eye's bulged, he pulled up the guitar, fumbled around with his trousers. Then I clearly heard him pull his flies up.

"What the fuck are you doing Aiden?" I shouted.

He stood up, balled his fists and hissed, "Calm down. I'm teaching her to play guitar."

"That's not what I'm talking about. What were you doing?"

Natty started crying.

"You want to watch what you say Skinner; Kipper won't like you upsetting his daughter," he stormed, retreating towards the patio doors.

"Natty it's alright," I said softly trying to calm her.

"You're not going to get away with this Aiden."

He barged out, shouting, "Huh, you don't know what you're talking about. You don't know anything … you're a fucking liar."

Now it all made sense, everything I'd seen over the last few months pointed to this. My guitar constantly being moved in my bedroom. Natty being so good on the guitar, despite having so few lessons, and most damning of all. Her not wanting to play guitar with me, because she thought I was going to do the same filthy fucking things as Aiden had been doing. For the life of me, I just hadn't been able to put the pieces together. Why? Because it was horrendous, unthinkable. Something nobody wanted to think about and no wonder. How could anyone do that? Who could do that? Only a fucking animal. Deep down inside, I felt I had played my part in it too. The abuse had happened right under my nose. With my fucking guitar being used as a prop. I'd been a cunt. Had been, but not now. There was no doubt in my mind I was going to do something. Whatever it fucking took. Slowly I moved towards her fragile convulsing frame.

"It's alright, Natty come on everything is going to be fine," I cooed.

"Nooooo."

"Please trust me, it's going to be fine. Everything is going to be OK. Where's mummy?"

"She's upstairs sleeping," she sobbed.

"Mummy will make it better I promise, now you wait here," I assured her, picking up the remote control and hitting the red button.

"Watch some TV while I go and talk to her, OK? I promise you it'll be fine. Shake on it?"

Natty swiped away her tears with the back of her hand then slowly nodded.

"Come on," I whispered softly, putting my hand out, and, after a long moment, she took it, gave it a shake, and then she turned her attention to the TV.

I ran upstairs taking two steps at a time and banged on Caitlin's bedroom door. "Caitlin, Caitlin, I need to talk to you," I cried.

She appeared, but she didn't look happy to be woken up. "What is it?" She asked impatiently.

"We need to talk now."

She swept the tangled hair from her face and yawned, "What's happened?"

"Look, it's…" I couldn't find the words, so I took her hand.

She wiggled free, "What have you done?"

"It's not me. Aiden's been at Natty," I spat.

She didn't say anything, she just stared at me.

"Did you hear me? That cunt Aiden has been abusing Natty."

"No, no. No way. Why do you say that?"

I told her what I had seen when I came in, but she shook her head, then a sinister look came over her face.

"I know what you're trying to do," she snarled, "You don't like Aiden, do you? You're trying to stitch him up."

"Oh, shut up, for fuck's sake. This isn't about me. Think about what you're saying. I wouldn't do that. I care about Natty; you must know that?"

"No, no, he wouldn't do that. I've known Aiden for years, we grew up together, we went to the same school," she said, nervously fiddling with her hair.

"Ask her. Protect your daughter."

She yelled, "I've been protecting my daughter for nine years now."

"What by shacking up with a fucking smack head?"

I knew I'd gone too far, but it was too late to take it back. She fell silent, she looked vulnerable, broken, washed out. Finished.

"Nobody wants me," she cried her voice trembling.

"Oh, come on, of course they do, don't say that."

"They don't," she sobbed wiping a tear from her cheek, "They find out who Natty's dad is, and they leave. They don't want me."

I took her hand again and squeezed it reassuringly.

"Forget everyone else for now just think of Natty, go and ask her."

She exhaled deeply, then dabbed at her face.

"Please Caitlin."

"You fucking better be right," she spat and went downstairs, while I went into my bedroom, sat on my bed and waited.

Even though the door was open, I couldn't hear what was being said, only the soft tone of Caitlin's voice as she tried to coax the truth from her daughter. A few minutes later, the front door slammed; now I was alone in the house. Where she was going, I didn't know, but I knew one thing. If Kipper found out about what was going on, he would hit first and ask questions later. It was time to start packing, get ready to go at a moment's notice. Grabbing my newspaper bag, I filled it with some clothes, my documents and passbooks. Whatever happened now, at least I was ready to go. Downstairs I heard the front door slam and then there were voices, so I crept to the top of the staircase and listened. It was Pete and Den.

Pete called up, "Skinner, there's something up with Den."

My first reaction was, I couldn't give a flying fuck, but Pete was a mate, and he sounded like he needed my help, so I went down to see what was going on. Den looked as bad as I'd ever seen him. His skin was grey. His body trembled. He used his arms to balance himself, and his bloodshot eyes were miles away.

Pete said, "I'm going to make him a cup of tea. You take him in the lounge, sit him in front of the fire, he's freezing."

Slowly, I led him into the living room to the settee, but he insisted on standing up.

"Kippers got Aiden," he told me, staring into the abyss.

"What?"

"Aiden's been touching up Natty, he's going to kill him," he said, scratching at his crusty beard, tears welling up in his eyes, "And I knew."

"Oh, come on Den, don't blame yourself. I was suspicious, deep down I suppose I knew too. I just couldn't…"

"No, I knew Skinner, I knew," he cut across me, "I caught him at it. He promised me, he wouldn't do it again. I couldn't do anything else; he was… Well, I couldn't do anything else."

"He was what? Sorting you out with your fucking smack?" I hissed, squaring up to him.

"I couldn't help it."

"You fucking bastard, you fucking bastard," I screamed.

"Go on then. Hit me."

I back handed him, splitting his top lip open,

"You piece of shit."

Den licked his lips, tasting the blood. Then he spat it in my face. That was it, I lunged at him, knocked him backwards onto the settee. Then I straddled him, holding him down. Before I knew what I was doing, my hands coiled around his neck and began to squeeze. It felt good. It felt like justice. His hands tugged at mine, but without any real conviction. It was like he wanted it. I wanted it. Both of us wanted it. My mind raced. Faces appeared, Natty's fearful and distraught, Caitlin's tearful and unbelieving, Kipper's laughing smashing cartilage and bone. There was only one thing that made any sense now. Crush the life out of the fucking cunt.

Pete bellowed, "Stop, Skinner, stop. You're going to kill him," pulling at my vice-like hands.

"Stop for god's sake stop!" He yelled.

"Fuck this, get your fucking hands off me," I shouted, hauling myself up.

Pete shouted back, demanding to know what happened, but I left the room, ignoring him. He'd have to wait. There was only one thing on my mind: To get - to Lenny's. Even before I knocked, I could hear screaming. Inside it made me shiver but made me feel good too. It was what the bastard deserved. On the second knock, Caitlin let me in, and I followed her into the living room. Aiden was lying spread eagled, pinned to the floor. Renny stood on his hands swinging a baseball bat menacingly, while Ridsey held his legs. Kipper loomed over him,

"Hold his eyes open Renny," he smirked rubbing the orange glowing end of his cigarette free.

Renny dropped down, dragged Aiden's eyelids upwards, then Kipper flicked the ember out of the cigarette into his eye.

Aiden writhed in agony, screaming, "No, please, please Kipper. I'm sorry it only happened one time, I'm sorry I'm sorry please no."

"Here give us another ciggy, Ridsey," he said turning, "Oh, Skinner, just in time for the show."

Aiden lifted his head, "Skinner? Skinner's the one who tried to score weed at your gaff in Harlow the night little Duggs got killed. It was him that you did time for."

Everything slowed down.

Kipper looked to Tracy, "You saw the cunt that night, didn't you Trace?"

Tracy gave me a cursory glance, "When he moved up here, I thought I'd seen him before, but I don't know."

"Caitlin? You used to hang around with Stampy's sister, she never stopped gabbing. She would have told you?" he snarled, turning his anger on her.

She stepped forward, "Don't you start on me Kipper."

"I asked you a fucking question you bitch."

She looked scared, then she steeled herself, shrugged, "Yeah, he was there. So what? It wasn't down to him. You killed that little kid; don't blame him."

Kipper jumped to his feet, "You're fucking dead punk; you owe me two fucking years."

Renny's baseball bat came down, glanced off his head and smashed onto his shoulder, sending him tumbling to the floor.

He shouted, "Run, Skinner," making for the patio doors.

Ridsey blocked my way, but he wasn't stopping me. Nobody was, especially that bastard. I smacked him a good one, and I ran out of the flat onto the Ridgeway. Paranoia raced through every part of me. Expecting to be hit at any moment, I kept on looking round. Then I lost my footing and fell headlong into the dirty grass. Checking behind again, I got up and ran with everything I had back to the flat. In the hall, I snatched up my crash helmet and my newspaper bag and ran to Black Death. She roared into life, and I shot off to the top of Longwood Road. I was about to turn right on the Ridgeway, away from Lenny's, when I saw something that resembled an old footstool lying in the grass. It had to be Stink, there was nothing else it could be. Without thinking I turned left towards Lenny's. There was no doubt about it. It was Stink alright. Coming up to him, I leant over, then grabbed him. He went fucking mad, barking, trying to bite me. So I dumped him into my newspaper bag and gave the bike plenty of throttle.

"It's alright boy I'm going to get you out of here."

Doggy was the only person I knew who would let me crash at his place at such short notice, so I headed for Thundridge, my old village. Thrashing Black Death all the way, I made the six-mile journey in record time. His house hadn't changed a bit since I'd left the village. So I parked up in my usual spot beside the pampas grass, switched off, then gently edged open my newspaper bag to check on Stink. He was in a bad way; he was unresponsive when I touched him. I shone my torch into the bag and saw the deep abrasions on his head were seeping. They looked like they'd gone septic. His breathing didn't sound right either. It was shallow and erratic like he was about to take his last. Time was of the essence.

"Hang on mate, you're going to be alright," I told him as I fast walked up Doggy's path.

Doggy must've seen me coming because he was waiting at the door, "Skinner, alright? Are you selling weights now?" He asked, viewing me through red eyes.

"What do you mean?"

"The bag, what's in the bag?"

I opened it.

"Very nice. A dead dog? Nice one," he frowned backing off.

"Nah, it's not dead, not yet anyway, he needs looking at, now. Listen, are the people who moved into my old house still there?"

"Who the Hamilton's? Yeah, I think so," he said with a grin catching on.

"Thank fuck for that, I'll be back in a minute."

Doggy nodded, "I'll get the bong ready," he called out.

"Yeah, you do that," I replied, running back to the VFR.

Nudging Stink to one side, I removed my documents from my bag, stuck them in my top box, and then I ran up the all too familiar road. In the dark, it was like nothing had changed. Even the light edging around the curtains from my old living room window was the same. I could've been walking up the road ten years ago. Soon, I was standing outside of the house. I took out a pen and a scrunched up old docket from my jacket pocket, wrote a few lines on it and attached it to Stink's collar. Doubled over I passed their car, and there it was on the back window, just as I remembered it from when they came to view the house. 'Beware of the Vet.' Back then, I thought it was pretty stupid, but now it was the best thing in the world.

I whispered, "It's going to be alright now mate," gently placing the bag on the doorstep,

"See you boy, good luck," I said, ringing the doorbell.

Immediately the porch light came on. I ran for the cover of the Holly tree I planted when I was five years old, and crouched down, watching and waiting. A few minutes later, an old woman with grey hair, opened the door.

"What on earth?" She exclaimed seeing the bag.

"What is it, Fran?" Said an elderly gentleman appearing beside her.

Fran leant forward, peeped in, "Oh my, it's a dog, there's a dog in there, is it dead Alan?"

Alan peered into the bag, "No, no it's still breathing, just, what's this?" He said plucking the note from Stink's collar and read,

"My name is Jeff. I've had a hard life. All I need is a chance."

Gently, Fran picked the bag up, "Come on, let's get him inside. The poor little mite."

"Goodbye Stinky Terrier. Long live Jeff," I whispered and the door clicked shut.

I felt something dripping on my hands. Through the dark green leaves of the Holly bush, I gazed up, scanning the sky for signs of rain, but it wasn't raining, I was crying. Crying for Natty, for Caitlin, for Cerys, Noel, Sulli and for the terrier. Crying for all the injustices in the world. For the life of me, I just couldn't work out why there was so much pain, so much anger, so much misery, on such a beautiful place as our Earth. It didn't make sense to me. How could it? It made no sense. On the way back, I pulled myself together, tried to think of positives, and by the time I'd got back to Doggy's I was ready for that bong, maybe a few. That's how it went for the next couple of days. In the evenings we'd do what we'd always done, get stoned and listen to music, but it didn't feel right, like I was just papering over the cracks. Returning was inevitable, I had to go back, I needed to know that Natty was OK, if Caitlin was alright, and what happened to Renny. Not knowing was a killer. Everything I'd worked for since leaving home was back on the Farm too. My clothes, my stack system and records, my amp, and most importantly, my flying V guitar. It wasn't a question of if. Just a question of when. On my way back from work, more than once, I had considered turning off the A10 at the Hertford junction and returning, but I'd put it off until the next day. Pressure built up. I felt like I was shitting out, letting other people suffer for something I had been a part of. In the end, there was no option, so I sat Doggy down, told him the full story. It was only fair because I wanted to borrow his car to get my stuff out. He wouldn't have it though. He said after what I had told him; he wanted to help me out. He would drive and help load my gear into the car. On the night of my return, Doggy and me stayed up late, watching *Monty Python's Life of Brian*. Although we were laughing at the silliness of it, both of us were feeling edgy, nervous about going. All too soon, the film ended, and that was it; we set off. Monday nights were always quiet on the Farm. Thankfully, this night was no different from any other. Doggy drove up and down Longwood Road a couple of times so we could check the place out. There was nobody about, and all the lights in the flat were off. It couldn't have been better. Doggy parked up at the bottom of my yard, and we cautiously weaved our way around the skeletal washing lines up to the front door.

"Fucking hell Doggy, look," I said, gesturing to the boarded-up windows.

"Hmmm. I wonder who did that?" Mumbled Doggy sarcastically.

He kept watch while I turned the key in the lock. The mortis dropped, the door cracked open, and we edged our way into the hall. It was freezing cold, like someone had forgotten to put the heating on. Kicking into something, I scanned the floor. As my eyes became accustomed to the light, I saw the hallway was strewn with rubbish.

The kitchen was the same. Everything had been turned upside down. Everything was decimated. It was like the storm had blasted its way through the downstairs. Doggy made for the stairs, indicating that we should get a move on.

Nodding in agreement, I traced his footsteps up, "Caitlin? Caitlin? It's Skinner," I called, when I got to the top of the stairs.

Hearing nothing, I followed Doggy into my bedroom, fearing the worst.

Doggy stopped, "Fucking hell."

My room had been tossed. I snatched up the few remaining undamaged albums from my wrecked stack system, and said, "Come on, let's get out of here."

"What about these T-shirts?" asked Doggy rummaging about in the chest of drawers.

"OK, yeah cheers mate, is the *Motörhead* one there?"

He held it up, then he put it over his shoulder with the others.

"What about your duvet and pillows?"

I reached down. They felt wet. I put my fingers to my nose. They smelt of piss.

"Doggy we're going now," I told him, already moving.

Near the bottom of the stairs, I heard music. It was my guitar.

Doggy blundered into the back of me. His voice low, he said, "Skinner, can you hear that?"

"Yeah," I said craning my neck around the banister.

Doggy pointed, "It's coming from the lounge," he hissed, but I was already on my way.

Slowly, I crept up to the door. Edged the handle down and straightaway, I smelt it. Something rotten, rancid. The music went up a notch, I pushed through into the room. The light came on. Kipper grabbed me by my lapels and smashed me against the wall.

"I knew you'd be back. Soppy cunt."

"What did I tell you Ridsey?" He laughed pushing his hands up around my throat.

"Yeah, you knew as always, Kip."

Hearing Ridsey's voice my eyes bulged. Kipper saw and cracked up,

"Everyone's here, look, all your mates," he said, shifting over.

Den was stretched out on the settee, Ridsey sat next to him, while the steroid bastard Jace was sitting in Pete's chair with my Flying V on his lap.

"You like Nirvana, Skinner?" He sneered standing up throwing the guitar above his head.

Ridsey smiled and sang, "Here we are now, entertain us."

Jace brought the guitar down on to the mantelpiece, splitting it down the middle.

Kipper smirked, "Behave yourself Jace. I was enjoying that," he laughed, then he turned his attention back to me.

"You owe me two years; do you know how much money I could make in two years?"

There was nothing I could do but shake my head.

"Nahhh, course you don't. Den owed me, didn't he Ridsey?"

Ridsey playfully slapped Den's lifeless face, and his head flopped to one side.

"Dennis couldn't pay. That's why he's a dead junkie cunt."

Jace nodded, "He spent all of Kipper's cash on brown."

Ridsey stood up grinning, then he tugged down his trackie bottoms.

"'Ere Den," he said, sitting down on his face, "Here's some brown for ya. Ya cunt."

They all cracked up laughing.

Kipper's laugh died in his throat, "You are going to do a wait and return for me aren't you?" he grinned, squeezing my throat on every word.

"Yeah, yeah, yeah," I said choking, trying to pull his hands off.

"Be here Saturday morning at 9 o'clock." He told me, letting go, "Go on then, fuck off."

Expecting to be jumped at any moment, I nervously made my way for the door.

Ridsey said, "He's thinking of not turning up, Kipper."

"Oh. He is," answered Jace.

I pulled down the handle on the front door, it clicked it open, and I felt the fresh air from outside.

Kipper called out, "Oh, by the way, how's Cerys? Does her family still live in Millfield?"

I stopped.

"Yeah, that's fucking right, be here at nine or we'll be at Millfield at ten."

THE DAM.

Amsterdam was the stoner's paradise according to Hippy John; he told me all about 'the Dam' when we worked on the archaeological digs around Ware and Hertford. What he said sounded amazing, but the truth was, he hadn't the words to describe how good it actually was. It wasn't just the quality of the weed or the number of shops, or even the decent people who frequented them. It was the other people, the other people of Amsterdam who were laid-back and accepted that some people liked to smoke herb. In the U.K. it was all so different. When I was fifteen, I smoked my first joint and people told me that I was a junkie; the very same people who were on the piss every night. Not only did I think they were hypocrites, I thought they needed to mind their own fucking business. In Amsterdam it wasn't like that, people were open-minded; if it was your thing, then that was up to you. I had come over on Saturday catching the noon ferry between Dover and Calais. On the way over the English Channel I'd been calm, relaxed even. It was an adventure. I didn't think about what lay in front of me, just sat back enjoying the sights and sounds of being at sea. No sooner than I'd got onto the roads of mainland Europe, I'd had to have my wits about me though. Driving on the right-hand side felt strange to start with. I had certainly raised a few eyebrows in Calais by turning onto side streets on the wrong side of the road, but away from the busy streets of the city, out on the motorways, it was a lot simpler. I just concentrated on the signs. Now and again as my mind drifted, I'd find it confusing seeing the cars on the other side of the motorway. It looked like it was a different road altogether. On the long straight motorways of Northern France, I'd made good time, then I crossed an unmanned checkpoint at the border and entered Belgium.

Belgium had been easy too: windmills, flatlands, and the Flanders fields, all faded into my rearview mirror at speeds of around 130 miles an hour. Holland had been much the same, but as I entered Amsterdam on the A4, I had to have my wits about me again. Every bone in my body was telling me to go one way, while the signs were telling me to go the other. Eventually, a brief encounter with a tram finally rammed the message home. I checked into a hotel in the centre near the Red-light district and the many Coffee Shops. I wasn't due to meet Kipper's contact until Sunday morning, so I had a quick shower, got a bite to eat and then hit Saturday night Amsterdam. It didn't take me long to find what I was looking for; the nearest Coffee Shop from my hotel was only a short walk away. Sauntering inside, I sat down and ordered 3.5g of Thai weed, just like I was ordering an English breakfast in a café back in London. The smoke was good and so was the atmosphere, so it wasn't long before I was sitting at a table with five or six other smokers, chatting, telling stories, making new friends. Everyone had a tale to tell; we sat back and listened as the spliffs went round and round the table. Then a couple of my new friends said they were going to take a look at the red-light district, and would I like to join them? I said why not. Spliffs sparking like torches leading the way, we entered De Wallen. I don't know whether it was the herb, but my first impression was that it was beautiful. Bars, Coffee Shops, and the luminescent blue windows with the working girls, threw their colourful lights onto the still surface of the canal at the middle of the strip. Enjoying the spectacle of it all, we wandered through the hordes of people to the girls in the windows. My initial feelings were, wow these girls are absolutely beautiful, but the more windows we passed, the less attractive they became. It was all a bit of a joke really. I was never sure what I thought about pornography. Obviously, as a kid it excited me. How could it not? It showed me things the media alluded to all the time, things I had never seen before. But as I grew older, saw the bigger picture, I started to believe that it was nasty and exploitative. Back in London with Geraldine, it didn't seem so bad because it was just one person, but here on the streets of De Wallen it was mass produced on an industrial scale. It was just another product; a commodity to be bought, and sold, like cattle, coffee, carrots or cotton.

In between the girls in the windows, there were sex shops, selling all kinds of products to get you off. I stopped to have a look and was accosted by someone offering to take us to a live sex show. Some of my new friends, including both of the girls, said yeah and disappeared into the bright lights, leaving me and a Polish bloke called Leon to find another Coffee Shop. Leon and me strolled on past several booths which were similar to pay toilets. I didn't know what they were, but Leon did, as he had tried one the previous day. He told me he went inside, put some money in a slot, the door locked, and a porno movie came on. He stressed it wasn't the start where the actors try to act. It was the latter part of the movie, maybe the last couple of minutes. He also said the floor in the booth was sticky because it was covered in spunk. Eyeing the passersby, I thought, what a bunch of wankers. Leon and me soon found another Coffee Shop, ordered, sat back, and waited for our other friends to return. A few minutes later, our order arrived: a nice bit of squidgy Black with a side order of Red Leb, and we got stuck in. Not long afterwards, our friends returned, saying they'd never do that again. I'm not sure what they were expecting, but the sex show was in another booth. It was bigger than the others, or 'the wank for one', as me and Leon were calling it, but it was the same principle. You'd go in, pay your money and the door would lock, but instead of a movie coming on, a window at the other side would open, revealing a couple cavorting on a bed. One of the girls said she was really enjoying it, that is, until she noticed that in one of the other windows there was an old man wanking furiously. Not for the first time, or the last, I looked at the passersby and thought, you wankers. In the small hours of the morning, I said goodbye to my new friends and made my way back to the hotel, feeling tired and not just a little bit stoned. Even though I tried not to think about why I was here, as I lay back on the bed, my thoughts turned to tomorrow. I couldn't settle for ages, then finally I dropped headlong into a fitful sleep. Seconds after I awoke, I knew there was something wrong; the noise outside told me the day had already begun. Begun a long time ago. I was supposed to meet Kipper's contact at noon and when I peered at the alarm clock on the bedside table, it told me it was noon. Sweeping the useless piece of shit onto the floor, I hauled myself out of bed, dressed quickly and got moving. Outside in the air, walking past the closed windows of the middle strip, I began to get my head together. The Thai grass had been strong, but thankfully, my instinct for survival was stronger. My confidence began to grow. Leon and me had walked past the Honour Bar the previous night, so I soon found the place. Skinheads wearing the standard garb of white T-shirts with red braces, blue jeans and ox blood red DMs stood outside, smoking and drinking. A few years earlier I would've been intimidated, but I didn't give a shit. It was just another youth culture. Plenty of Skins liked punk and spliff. They went to the same gigs as me, so I confidently strolled in and gave the Skin-girl behind the bar a nod. She nodded back, said something in Dutch.

"Is Erik about?" I asked.

A couple of Skins looked around, interested in the stranger.

"Who's asking?" She effortlessly switched to English.

"Kipper."

Nodding she said, "One moment please," and left.

"Are you English?" Asked one of the Skins standing next to me.

"Yeah," I said giving him the once over. He was small, wiry, dressed in standard issue, DM boots, braces, white stay pressed shirt and green Harrington.

"English," he repeated, giving me a big smile, making sure I saw his teeth.

Silver fronts, like the bloke Jaws in the James Bond movie, *Moonraker,* glinted back at me. Keeping the silver on show, he threw his hand out for me to shake, but as I put my hand in his, he gripped my fingers hard trying to crush them. People had done this before, many times, and everyone who had done it was a cunt as far as I was concerned, but I let him squeeze away none the less. If I was going to stand up for myself, I'd pick my battles. It would be for a good reason, not just some dickhead trying to intimidate me with a silly handshake.

"What football team do you support?" He asked, letting go.

"Here. We are all Ajax," he challenged.

"I'm not into football mate," I told him, quite truthfully.

He seemed confused, then he laughed, "Ajax are the best Europe team, better than your English teams."

Shrugging my shoulders, I turned my attention to the bar, hoping that the bore would fuck off, and the Skin-girl would fucking come back.

"You are a biker, no?" He persisted, placing his hand on my shoulder.

"I have a Yamaha Ténéré... This is a superior motorcycle."

Nodding with a straight face, I said, "Woww," showing my contempt.

"My motorcycle will beat any motorcycle," he boasted, still on the wind up.

"Is that right?" I yawned.

"Pick a card," he told me, slapping a pack of cards onto the bar.

"Nah, I'm busy man, maybe later yeah?" I told him, getting riled.

"Pick a card now, just one," he insisted, cutting the cards.

I rounded on him and snarled, "Piss off you wanker."

He smirked and opened his Harrington, showing me the butt of a gun.

"Whoa," I said backing off.

"Yes, English," he snapped through his metallic fronts.

"Christian, stop annoying our guest," joked another Skin from behind the bar.

Christian smiled at his mate and zipped up his Harrington.

"I'm Erik, and your name is?" He said, approaching me but still eyeing Christian.

Keeping my building resentment at bay, I told him who I was, who sent me and where I had come from. Satisfied with my answers, he asked me for the letter. I fumbled it out of my back pocket, handed it over, then waited while he read it, keeping one eye on Jaws. Again satisfied, he flipped up the hatch on the bar, indicating that I should follow him.

Before we left the bar, Erik winked at Christian and laughed, "You will behave yourself."

Erik led the way along a corridor into a small room and told me to sit down while he opened a small safe in the corner. He produced a package about the size of a brick and handed it over to me with a menacing look on his face.

"Look after this with your life."

Nodding, understanding all too well, what was expected of me, I eased the package into the inside pocket of my jacket, and followed him back into the bar. Erik offered me a drink on the house before my journey back, but I politely refused. Too right I did, I wanted to get out of there as soon as possible. Not only did I want to get the package back to the relative safety of my hotel room, I needed to get the fuck away from the metal mouthed dickhead with the gun.

Erik said, "Greetings to Kipper," while Christian's eyes followed me out of the bar.

Now the pick up had been done, I began to relax as I made my way through the throngs of people along the strip. In the daylight it seemed even more ridiculous. Scantily clad, shark eyed women touted themselves for business from behind the thick glass. On the other side, punters looked on with cold clinical faces weighing up the potential purchase. I must've been about halfway along the strip when I noticed Christian following. The fucking prick was blatant, hardly bothering to hide himself. Speeding up, I dropped down onto my haunches, hoping to lose him, but he soon caught sight of me again. I thought if I was going to lose him, it would be by staying in the crowds. Switching, I doubled back to where my friends had seen the live sex shows. Dodging inside one, I put my money in the slot and the door locked behind me. The window opened revealing two girls on the bed doing a 69er. In fascination, I watched as they delicately lapped one another. Then opposite, the window opened. Christian's metallic grin gleamed in the darkness. I sprinted out, but instead of running back down the strip, I dived into one of the 'wank for one' booths. Needing to get the door locked quickly, I stepped forward to pay and almost skidded over on the cum encrusted floor. In front of me, the grainy screen flickered to life. There was a young girl giving a guy a blow job. Almost immediately, he came on her face. Then another one. Then another one. Then another one. Then another one. I was going out of my mind; I was going fucking mental. It had to stop, but it didn't. I went for the door handle, but the thought of Christian made me change my mind, so with no option I turned back to the screen. It carried on just as before. Then I realised something. What I'd thought of earlier on as a bit of fun and a laugh had more sinister connotations. In these movies, women were just rubbish, to be abused, knocked about, to become cum receptacles for their masters. Finally, the booth fell into darkness as it timed out and the door unlocked. Immediately, it flew open. I balled my fist, drew my arm back, ready to knock that gun toting cunt out, but it was only another punter. Exchanging a glance, I then elbowed past him, back out into the crowds, watching for Christian, but I couldn't see him anywhere. Keeping myself with the flow of people, I made my way out of the red-light district and back to the hotel. No sooner had I shut the door, I felt safe. Somehow, being up high on the fifth floor made me feel safer still. Even though my ferry wasn't due to leave for the U.K. until the next morning, I was still jumpy after what had happened. I couldn't sit down, so I thought I'd prepare for the return trip. I had thought it through on my last night at Doggy's. I removed the brick like package from my inside pocket, then laid my leather jacket on the bed upside down and placed it on top. Then I took my flick knife and carefully dug into the plastic, trying not to spill any. Eventually I saw the white powder within, so I dabbed a bit on my finger and rubbed it on my teeth. My mouth soon became numb. It was cocaine alright. I then picked out the spoon from my toolbox on the bedside table and began to fill up the extra strong condoms I had brought on the strip. It was a laboriously slow task. It took ages, but when I finished, I had twelve coke filled condoms lying on the bed. Now I had to do the thing, the thing that I was least looking forward to. I lifted up one of the bloated condoms, dipped it in olive oil, put it into my mouth and tried to swallow. Immediately I began to retch. It was stuck in my throat. Unable to breathe, I grabbed the tie and tried to pull it out, but the gossamer rubber stretched and kept on stretching. Fear rose up inside me. I thought the fucking thing is going to burst, I'll die of an overdose. If it doesn't, I'm going to fucking die of asphyxiation. Do something. Do something now. Snatching up the bottle of olive oil, I ran into the bathroom and poured the rest of it into my mouth, gave the tie another tug and the bastard plopped onto the floor. Panting like a fucking dog on a hot day, I looked down into the sink at the oily condom thinking, I'm going to have to try something else; I can't even do one, let alone twelve. Back in my room, I sat down on the bed trying to think of a solution to the problem. Then I saw a shadow at the window. There was somebody standing at the window, looking in at the row of cocaine filled condoms on my bed. For the life of me, I couldn't understand what was going on. My room was up on the fifth fucking floor. What was the guy doing? Fucking levitating. Bouncing up, I rushed to the window and threw the curtains closed. A few moments passed. Then I peeped through the gap and saw there was a walkway. I couldn't fucking believe it. How could I not have seen that? That was it. Even though I'd planned to go out with Leon, I decided it was time to make a run for it. I could ride back to Calais and stay there before I took the ferry home the next day. It made sense to me, but I still had the problem of finding a way to smuggle the coke into the U.K. There was no way I was going to try and take it through customs relying on them not stopping me. Even if I wasn't breaking the law, the authorities in the U.K. always stopped me. In the end, it was simple, so simple that I wondered why I hadn't thought of it in the first place. I went to a garage, bought a five litre can of oil and sneaked it back up into my room. I carefully opened it, trying to keep the plastic retainer under the lid intact, and poured it down the toilet. By the time I drained about half the can, the toilet was broken. Now I really have got to get out of here, I thought. Once the can was empty, I filled it about halfway up with water from the tap, then brought it back into the bedroom. Condoms float in water, so I tied them to some spanners from my toolbox, then, one by one, eased them gently into the oil can. It looked perfect; the weighted condoms had sunk and because the can was still thick with oil, the freshly added water looked like oil. For the finishing touch, I took the little plastic retainer and meticulously glued it back onto the can, so it looked like it hadn't been opened. I was ready to go. For some unknown reason, I put my hand on the Gideon Bible on the bedside cabinet, then made my way to the door. There was a knock. I froze. It came again but more insistent. Fuck it, fuck off, I thought, making my way over to the spy hole. It was Leon. I snatched the door open.

"You alright Leon?" I said, rounding him.

"Hello Mr, popular," he smiled, "What's your hurry?"

"I need to go."

"Are you leaving us?" He frowned, noticing that I had all of my gear with me.

"Sorry Leon, I need to go, mate."

"Are you sneaking out without paying?" He whispered.

"Yeah, yeah, yeah, something like that," I said, hurrying down the corridor towards the lift.

"Amsterdam is not this kind of place; this is very rude. You don't pay your bill. You don't say goodbye to me and leave with other friends."

The lift was on the ground floor, so I jabbed at the button.

"What other friends?" I murmured absently.

"Your friends in reception," he explained.

"What did they look like?" I asked. But deep down I already knew.

"Oh, these are two Skinheads, one had silver for teeth."

The lift was now making its way up from the ground floor.

"Cheers Leon," I thanked him, abandoning the lift and heading for the stairs, with my heart thumping in my chest.

Bouncing down the stairs three steps at a time, I drove myself to the limit. Then when I got to the bottom, I peered through a reinforced glass window into reception. Christian and a fat Skinhead stood chatting with the receptionist. She nodded and started checking the hotel's register. For the life of me, I didn't know what to do. I was knackered out, panting hard, then I saw the fire door. With no other option, I barged through. Immediately, the fire alarm went off, wailing, alerting everyone that someone was trying to sneak out of the hotel. I legged it into the hotel's car park to Black Death. There was shouting behind me, but it was drowned out by my roaring engine. Kicking the bike down into first gear, I turned and saw the silhouette of someone levelling a gun at me. Bullets fizzed past my head, hitting the pillar next to me throwing up dust. I opened the throttle and powered over to a row of cars in the middle, trying to get some cover. Windows shattered, showering glass. Christian kept on coming.

"Peeka-boo, you fuck you," he screamed at the top of his voice.

Christian was never going to stop; he was like a robot. It was shit or bust. I made my move, darting for the exit, but the barrier was down, so I weaved the bike through the pedestrian entrance and out on to the street. People started shouting and waving at me. I wondered what was going on, until a tram came hurtling in my direction. Dropping my shoulder, I swerved around it and found myself in the path of an oncoming car. Lights blazing, horn blasting, it wasn't changing direction. It just kept coming. This time, I cut to the right and jolted up on to the pavement. Now completely out of control, the VFR smashed through a group of skeletal black bicycles, then juddered to a halt. Behind me, the tram and the cars had all stopped. People had stopped too. They were staring in my direction. Only one thing was moving on the street. It was going the wrong way, like I had been. It was a bike. It was a Ténéré. It had to be him. Carrying on down a one-way street in the wrong direction wasn't an option, so I looked about for another escape route. The only thing I could see was a small, up and over pedestrian bridge.

The Ténéré was approaching fast. Kicking down, I wound my way out of the mangled bike frames and gave it maximum throttle. I raced at the bridge and a figure appeared. I leant hard left, missed the figure and hit the bridge doing 50 MPH. The bike took off. It sailed through the air. Then dumped me down on a walkway full of people. No way was I stopping though. Keeping my head low, I kept the horn blaring, warning them to get out of the fucking way. They shouted, screamed, then jumped out the way; some of them tried to hit me as I parted them. Soon, I made it to the end of the walkway, and finally, came to a road. Hardly daring to look, I glanced over my shoulder. There was nobody there. I had lost him. Breathing a huge sigh of relief, I kicked Black Death down into first gear and shot off. Destination Calais.

OVER AND OUT.

Bow doors crashed, the ferry shook, voices rang out, then the first line of cars moved off. This was it. This is what I had been dreading yet waiting for. Whatever happened in the next hour could change my life; change it forever. Nearly every street in the West End had its homeless. Sometimes when the radio went quiet, I wondered what had brought them here. Why were they there? Could it be bad luck? Bad decisions? Mental health? Or was it all down to one great big fucking mistake? Engines started around me, so I hit my start button. Black Death roared into life beneath me. Pulling away, I carefully followed the car in front across the deck, then bounced up the gang plank onto solid ground. I was back in England. The snake-like line of cars crept up to the passport office. Windows dropped open; passports were shown. Then the cars continued towards the exit. Firstly, I couldn't believe what I was seeing, surely it couldn't be this easy. Inside, my excitement built up in an incredible rush. Maybe they weren't checking cars today, maybe there was a strike. Maybe I was just a lucky bastard. I showed my passport, received a tired nod for my trouble and joined the cars making their way towards the exit. I thought, I'm going to make it, it's going to be OK, I'll never do this again. I swear. But as we came up to the perimeter fence, the markings on the concrete directed us away from the exit, back into the docks, back towards the customs and excise checkpoint. My head dropped. My heart rate picked up. Slowing down to a roll, I looked left and right, checking to see if there was any other way out, but there wasn't. I just had to follow the car in front. One by one, the cars were waved through. Then a customs officer craned his neck, casting his eyes back along the queue, saw me, looked at his compatriot, and nodded. Physically, I began to fall apart. My heart rate intensified. My breathing became laboured. Panic set in. I had been right; I'd fallen at the first hurdle; I'd been a fucking idiot. My naïve show of emotion at Calais had given the game away, like I knew it had. Now all that was left to cling onto was the confidence in how well I'd hidden the cocaine. And that wasn't much. Even before I'd got close to the customs officer, he stepped out, confidently put his hand up and waved, directing me into what I could only describe as a warehouse. Inside the vast expanse of metal, it was empty apart from a couple of cars left unattended in the middle. Next to a car ramp, stood two uniformed officers who beckoned me over. I pulled up, hauled Black Death up onto its centre stand and shakily removed my crash helmet. Both greeted me with a good afternoon, and I gave them a cursory nod in return. One of them had a red face and the other, obviously the more senior, had a square jaw. Both looked professional, relaxed and in control, like this was their environment, and they were successful in it. The officer who directed me into the warehouse shut the outside door with a crash. It looked like I was the only one that had been pulled out of the queue.

"Right, just a couple questions before we get started. Can you tell us where you've been?"

Questioned Square Jaw, picking up his clipboard and pen.

"Antwerp," I said, scratching at the stubble on my chin.

"And what was your business in Antwerp?"

"I'm a despatch rider; I had a delivery there."

"Despatch rider," he repeated carefully jotting it down.

"Right, go and sit over there," he nodded to a row of chairs, "we're just going to have a look at your bike."

"Yeah, OK, you won't be long, will you?" I said, sitting down hard, feeling lightheaded.

"We'll be as long as it takes," he replied belligerently.

Butterflies gnawed at my stomach, my heart pounded like it was going to burst, my chest heaved up and down, trying to get enough oxygen, but no matter how much it heaved, it wasn't enough. It felt like I was being smothered. I just hoped that nobody could see my discomfort.

Both officials stood back talking for a while, pointing at different areas of Black Death. Then the search began. Red Face opened the top box, lifted out the oil can, carefully put it to one side and began going through the top box. I couldn't fucking believe it; he hadn't even looked at it. Deep down I was singing, I wanted to jump up and down laughing at the stupid fucking tosser, but any sign of emotion would be repeating my earlier mistake. Now that would've been fucking stupid. If I had learnt one thing on this trip, it was not to show people how I was feeling. Red Face spent ages rummaging around, desperately trying to find something incriminating. Finding nothing, he walked straight past the oil can to a bench covered in tools, picked up a torch and returned. I watched in wonder. He lay down under the bike, switched on the torch and began checking inside the bottom of the fairing. Meanwhile Square Jaw had emptied my throw-over panniers onto the bench and was carefully sifting through its contents with his pen. A few minutes later, satisfied there was nothing of interest inside, he shoved my gear back in and dropped the throwovers off next to the oil can on his way back to the bike. He went around the front and rooted around in one of my handlebar mitts. He frowned, drew something out, turned it over in his hand and showed it to Red Face, who nodded. What it was I didn't know, but it couldn't be good because Square Jaw was looking extremely pleased with himself as he approached.

"Can you explain this?" He asked triumphantly, holding up a parking ticket from Amsterdam.

The first thing that came to mind was, "I've got a girlfriend in Amsterdam, she's a prostitute."

He nodded, frowned, then shrugged his shoulders, "But why did you say that you'd been in Antwerp?"

"I'm not proud of it, you know... It's not a nice thing, is it?"

"Why would I care? And..."

"It's not something I tell people."

"No, no, I'm not having that. You've got something and we're going to find it," he retorted irritably and marched to the bench.

He snatched up a tool kit, marched over to Black Death, knelt down and unscrewed the seat. Then he ripped it out of its housings, checked underneath and then started to remove the petrol tank. That was it, enough was enough, I jumped up and pounded over to them.

"You better not fuck my bike up."

Square Jaw looked up, his mouth gaping,

"Go and sit back down."

"If you damage it, you'll fucking pay for it," I told him, raising my voice.

"Sit down," he returned, "or I'm going to call the police."

"You're wasting your time! I haven't got anything," I shouted.

"One last chance. Sit down."

"For fuck's sake, if I was going to smuggle something do you think I'd use a fucking motorbike?" I snarled as I strode away.

Red Face picked up a telephone on the bench while Square Jaw looked on. It was a long call; they had another trick up their sleeve. No doubt about it. Finally, he put the phone down, said something to Square Jaw who nodded tempestuously. He then lowered himself back down onto his knees and started putting my bike back together again. A few minutes later it was done, and the two officials stood back scanning the bike. Now and again, one of them would take the torch and shine it on the VFR scanning for something, anything, but it looked like they were waiting on someone. Red Face began to make a cup of tea, and I thought fuck this, I've had enough, this bullshit is over. I started to get up, but quickly sat back down, when a sniffer dog trotted into the warehouse, heading towards Black Death. Suddenly, all my bravado was gone. I'm sure I grimaced but everybody was so intent on watching the little dog. Wagging its tail enthusiastically, it trotted straight past the oil can, and up to the bike, took a few sniffs, looked lovingly up at its handler and moved on to some more interesting smells under the bench.

Not for a second time, did I resist the urge to jump for joy, laugh and take the piss out of the stupid fuckers. They were a bunch of clowns. Square Jaw walked up, indicating to me to put my arms out to the side so he could do a body search. I couldn't help myself, I just laughed in the silly bastards face.

He knew that he was wasting his time, so he gave me a quick pat down, "I know you've got something," he told me.

"Oh no I haven't," I pantomimed back, grinning at Red Face, as he carefully put the oil can loaded with cocaine back into my top box.

"My advice to you is, don't come back through here again, we will get you."

"Oh no you won't."

Square Jaw moved aside before I knocked into him, and I made my way back over to the bike, gave it a quick inspection myself, jumped on and turned it over. Probably not the brightest thing to do under the circumstances, but as I left the warehouse, I gave the two of them the wankers sign. I couldn't help it. They were so fucking stupid they couldn't find a kilo of cocaine hidden on a motorbike. Slowly, I rode out of the port, enjoying my little victory, knowing that this wasn't over, there could be worse to come. Kipper had told me to call him as soon as I was back in England, so he could give me an address for where to drop the kilo. I was knackered after the last couple of days riding, but I'd rather have ridden to Inverness than gone to the Farm and dealt with that bastard. A few miles down the seafront road I spotted a phone box, pulled over, jumped off

Black Death, fumbled a ten pence coin from my pocket and went in. Dialling Lenny's place, I inhaled deeply. The phone beeped and I rammed in my 10p.

Tracy always answered the phone at Lenny's, so I said, "Hello, Tracy?"

"Skinner?" A familiar voice called out from the other end of the line enthusiastically.

"Renny, fucking hell man, where's Kipper?"

"He's gone Skinner, the old bill picked him up, he's been nicked for murder."

"Fucking hell," I said, sweeping my hand back through my matted hair.

"Aiden's gone too; he got arrested in hospital last night. Indecent assault on a minor."

"What about Caitlin and Natty? Are they alright?"

"Yeah, yeah. Considering everything, they're OK. They're staying at Hippy John's until they can get something permanent."

"Thank fuck for that," I said, hearing the phone start to beep, "Right mate, I better get going. I'll see you soon."

"Hold on, hold on, did you pick up something in Holland?"

I chuckled, "Yeah. I did, it's in my top box."

"Come on back mate, we're going to be fucking rich!" he laughed, and the line went dead.

"Rich, yeah," I said putting the receiver down and I eased open the door.

In front of me, the sun's rays drew a shimmering pathway across the surface of the English Channel. Seagulls careered in the blue skies above while higher up, cotton wool clouds scudded in from the West. I felt at one with the world, at peace, part of a bigger picture. It was time to go home. Black Death roared into life underneath me, I kicked down and shot off through the streets of Dover. Now the roads were back to normal, I grabbed even more throttle. To the left, the sea dropped away as I raced up the steep cliff roads. Then at the top, Dover gave way to the rich green fields of Kent. The countryside welcomed me back like an old friend. I opened the bike up, leant forward and checked the clock. Black Death's speedo showed me I was doing 150 miles an hour. One mistake now and I'd be dead. I've never felt so alive.

COMING NEXT

THERE'S ALWAYS ANOTHER DAY IN COLOMBIA.

'BLISTERING ROAD TRIP OF COCAINE, CARTELS AND CHICAS.'

Printed in Great Britain
by Amazon